A DAUGHTER
of the
CONFEDERACY

Lauraine White

Cover Design: Ivy & Bees
Interior Design: KUHN Design Group | kuhndesigngroup.com
Publisher: Miracle Movement
Editorial Consultant: Dabian Witherspoon

LIMITS OF LIABILITY AND DISCLAIMER OF WARRANTY

WARNING – DISCLAIMER

DAUGHTER OF THE CONFEDERACY

ISBN for print: 979-8-9903849-6-5
ISBN for digital copy: 979-8-9903849-7-2

Books may be purchased by contacting the publisher and author at: miracle-movement.com

www.miracle-movement.com

DEDICATION

To my ancestors—both named and unnamed, both remembered and deliberately erased—I dedicate this work. To those who were bought and sold like property yet endured with unbreakable spirit, we see you. To those who sang while in chains, who prayed in the shadows, and who dared to dream beyond the fields they were forced to labor—we hear you. Your blood runs through these pages. Your legacy lives in every word.

This is for you.

This is for the grandmothers, whose backs bore the weight of empire, and the grandfathers whose dignity was never up for auction. This is for the babies buried in unmarked graves, and the warriors who lived long enough to pass down a song, a scar, or a scripture.

Your blood speaks. Your resilience rises. Your legacy lives—in me, and through these pages.

This is not just my story. This is yours. And I will not let the world forget you.

CONTENTS

CONTENTS

THE TIES THAT STILL BIND

"We hold these truths to be self-evident, that all men are created equal, that they are endowed by their Creator with certain unalienable Rights, that among these are Life, Liberty and the pursuit of Happiness."[1]

These words are etched into the foundation of a nation that has never fully lived them out. They were penned by men who claimed liberty while holding others in chains—men who declared freedom while denying it to those whose skin bore the evidence of another story entirely. These words, lofty and noble, became the gospel of American exceptionalism. But for those of us born from the bloodlines of the enslaved, they have always read more like prophecy than history—longed for, but not yet fulfilled. *A Daughter of the Confederacy* was born from this tension.

This book was never meant to be easy, and I did not set out to write it to fit neatly into a single genre. Because nothing about the story of this nation—or my place within it—has ever been neat.

The story of *A Daughter of the Confederacy* came to me not as a complete vision, but in fragments—memories not my own, echoes passed down

---

1. Continental Congress. The U.S. Declaration of Independence (1776).

through silence, census records, oral histories, and the aching questions I could no longer ignore. I searched for names that were lost, voices that were silenced, and moments of love that bloomed in impossible places. What I found was more than history—it was inheritance.

To write this book, I walked through archives and prayed over plantation records. I read letters between Confederate officers and counted the names of enslaved people listed not as humans, but as property. I examined the redlining maps that shaped our neighborhoods, the laws that reshaped our families, and the generational lies that reshaped our faith. I also sat with Scripture—especially the stories of deliverance, of exodus, and of prophetic courage. It was there I was reminded: God has always been on the side of the oppressed.

A Daughter of the Confederacy is, in many ways, a layered offering. It is a family history passed down in whispers and stares, in unmarked graves and unnamed fathers. It is a love story—tender and defiant—between two people who dared to feel what the world told them they had no right to feel. It is historical fiction, pieced together from fragments of research and the fabric of my own imagination. It is also a memoir—my reflection on inheritance, identity, and the war still waging in the marrow of this nation's bones.

I wrote this for those whose stories were buried underneath plantations and policies. It is for the voices choked out by the noose of whitewashed textbooks and silenced by Southern pride parading as heritage. I wrote it for the Black mothers whose lullabies carried their children through horror. It is for the daughters and sons of the enslaved and the enslavers—because whether we choose to claim it or not, that blood still runs in our veins. Mine too.

In the pages ahead, you will meet Hilliard and Emma. Though the story line is fictional, their truth rises from real soil—rooted in Letohatchee, Alabama, where my ancestors once walked and toiled, loved and suffered.

Hilliard was the white son of an enslaving plantation owner of Confederate lineage. Emma was a Black woman born into bondage on his family's land. Their love, impossible, was never meant to survive in a country that profited from their division. Their bond, unbreakable, yet their story is proof that even in soil poisoned by slavery and silence, love can still take root. Through them, I explore what it means to be family in a land that was built to keep us apart.

This book is a love story, yes—but not just between Hilliard and Emma. It is a love story between truth and history, between justice and memory.

It is a family story—mine, and perhaps yours too. It's told through fiction shaped by research, and through reflection shaped by faith.

It is a God-breathed work, and is told in the raw, redemptive power of truth. The kind of truth that Jesus said would set us free. This is the kind of truth that does not flinch in the face of injustice—it confronts it boldly and speaks with unwavering authority. It is the kind of truth that exposes sin, not only the sins of individuals, but the deeply embedded sins of systems. Not only the sins of the past, but the ones still breathing in the present.

It is a message of reckoning. It is a sacred unveiling. It is a confrontation with the sin of America's original lie: that some lives matter more than others.

This is also my story. It is a mirror held up to my lineage, my faith, my Blackness, and my Southern roots. I write as a daughter of the Confederacy—not by allegiance, but by inheritance. It is not because I align myself with the ideology of that rebellion or its defeat, but because I am one of its tangled descendants. I carry both the trauma and the triumph of a land that loved its monuments more than its people. I come from both sides of the color line. And because of that, I write not just to remember—but to redeem.

This book is an indictment of a nation that has muted Black voices while magnifying the myths of white glory. It is a challenge to the edited history that made heroes of enslavers and footnotes of the enslaved. It is a call to reclaim what was buried—not only in books, but in blood. Because the truth is this: whether by blood, by bond, or by brutal history, *we are family*. And family, no matter how fractured, must face itself to be made whole.

So, this is not just a book. It's an unveiling. It is an incrimination and an invitation. A reckoning and a release.

I invite you to read it with an open heart and an unguarded soul. To trace the lines of fiction until you find the truth from which they were drawn. To listen for the echoes of your own story—because if you live in this country, you are in this book too.

So let this be our confession—a truth we will no longer deny or dilute. And let it also be our commitment—a vow to live differently because we now see clearly.

We hold these truths to be self-evident—but they have never been self-executing. It's time we live them. It's time we tell the truth. It's time we write a new story—together. *And let the healing begin—where the roots run deepest.*

—*Lauraine White*

I

WHO'S YOUR DADDY?

The land remembers who built it—
and who was buried beneath it.

Have you ever watched a tea kettle just before it whistles? It is silent—until it's not. The boiling point builds quietly, unseen, until the pressure inside can no longer be contained. There's a moment—a subtle shift—when you sense something is about to break. The water beneath the surface is bubbling, the steam is pressing against the lid, and then it happens. A high-pitched scream pierces the air. That high-pitched whistle isn't just a signal for tea—it's a warning. It's the kettle's way of saying, *Enough. The pressure is too much. Something needs to break free.*

That sound is a signal. A boiling point. A release. A warning. A demand for action.

Right now, the world is at that boiling point. The pressure of history, silence, and injustice has reached its breaking. The whistle is blowing and screaming in our ears, but too many have trained themselves to tune it out. They are conditioned to numbness and wrapped in apathy.

We have seen the warning signs before—those kumbaya moments that called us to unity, when people held hands and sang hope-filled songs beneath banners proclaiming progress. But when the music faded and the rallies dispersed, we returned. We returned to what we called "normal." We returned to silence. We went back to sleep. We have become far too skilled at going back to what is familiar—at numbing ourselves with the language of unity and the symbols of progress that soothe the soul yet never dare to transform the systems that continue to wound it.

One of those moments of "almost" was the election of President Barack Obama. For some, it felt like redemption—evidence that America had finally moved beyond its darkest sins. But it wasn't quite what it seemed. America had not healed. It had learned how to perform.

President Obama was the perfect performance piece: biracial, articulate, calm, and charismatic. He was someone white America could embrace without confronting its own reflection. He carried the ancestry of both the oppressed and the oppressor—and it made him a satiable answer to a centuries-old problem. He was, in many ways, their bridge—someone who carried both lineages, and yet didn't fully belong to either.

He wasn't too loud. He wasn't too angry. He wasn't *too* black. He was palatable. He fit into a version of the American Dream that comforted those who wanted change, but not accountability. His story was elegant, even tragic—especially with the passing of his white grandmother just before his election, giving the nation a shared grief they could all feel safe embracing.

But in the shadows, something ancient stirred. America's other legacy—it's more deeply rooted one—began to rattle.

It's what has always made America "great" in the eyes of those invested in its dominance: its unrepentant disdain for Blackness. The very fact that a Black man would live in the White House as President—an institution never meant for his kind—shook the foundation. It didn't just inspire; it offended. It pulled back the curtain on a truth many still try to deny. The whispers of America's past turned into a roar, and the backlash came like a tidal wave.

That house wasn't just white on the outside. It was built, brick by brick, to uphold whiteness. For them, it represents preservation—of whiteness, of privilege, of a system built on supremacy. And anything that challenged that, anything that attempted to redefine it—was always going to be seen as a threat.

Then came May 25, 2020. The whistle blew again. This one shrieked through screens and speakers across the world when George Floyd was murdered in broad daylight. The world watched as the breath was forced from his lungs. We watched, not in passing, but in lockdown—because COVID-19 had paused everything else. We couldn't turn away.

The murder of George Floyd was not the first. It wasn't the most violent. It wasn't the most gruesome. But it was the one the entire world couldn't turn away from. This time, something shifted. Because in a twist only God could orchestrate, the entire planet had been brought to a halt by a virus. People were home. Eyes were glued to screens. Hearts were still enough to *see*.

And what they saw was America's sickness, stripped bare. God had already marked the moment.

George Floyd's death coincided with sacred moments on God's calendar—Shavuot for the Jews, Pentecost for the Christians. These are not accidental alignments. Shavuot marks the giving of the Torah on Mount Sinai after God parted the Red Sea to deliver His people, thereby sealing His covenant with them. Pentecost commemorates the outpouring of the Holy Spirit on believers, empowering them to speak, move, and act with divine authority. The common thread that weaves these two occurrences is God giving His people instructions.

Why would a moment of racial injustice be tied to such holy ground? Because God speaks through signs and He marked that day. It was not just as another tragedy, but as a spiritual reckoning. A reminder. It was a confrontation with the covenant He still holds with the oppressed and forgotten.

God does not forget covenant. And when His covenant people cry out—when the oppressed can no longer breathe—He responds. He exposes. He disrupts. He makes sure the world watches.

As Scripture says in 1 Corinthians 1:27-29 (AMP): *"But God has selected [for His purpose] the foolish things of the world to shame the wise… the weak things… the insignificant, the despised… so that no one may boast in the presence of God."*

This was that moment. It was a divine dismantling and a season of godly sorrow.

For me, the seeds of this revelation were planted long before that day. In 2011, during a family reunion on my mother's side, the conversation turned to ancestry. My curiosity was piqued. The stories passed down through generations—whispers about a white great-great-grandfather—needed answers. So, I searched. What I found would change me.

Our family's history wasn't just folklore. It was documented. What I found was more than history. It was prophecy. My great-great-grandfather, Hilliard J. Whitley, was a white man who married a Black woman named Emma—his family's slave. According to the records, they weren't just lovers. They were siblings. They had the same father but different mothers.

The year was pre-Civil War. It was in Letohatchee, Alabama—between Montgomery and Selma. A Southern landowner's son chose love over legacy. He defied everything his lineage stood for. He dared to marry a woman who was not only enslaved but also his blood. He loved her and it cost him everything.

His mother disowned him. His father moved away in shame after his mother's death. His brother went on to be a decorated Confederate soldier and later a senator. But Hilliard? He was erased. He was labeled, rejected, forgotten, and dismissed as nothing more than a traitor to whiteness—a "nigger lover" in the cruelest of terms. He dared to cross a line written in the blood of the Confederacy.

Would a man really give up everything for love? And how could he, at the same time, be both beneficiary and betrayer of a system designed to destroy the woman he loved? What could make a man give up his inheritance, his status, and his family's name—for a woman, the world said was less than human?

That question still haunts me. Hilliard's story is more than personal—it's generational. That contradiction—of loving a Black woman while living off the profits of Black suffering—is America's story. It's in our roots. It's in our laws. It's in our institutions. It's in the DNA of those who built fortunes on backs like mine, while claiming moral high ground. A man torn between love and legacy, between truth and tradition, and between justice and justification.

And we ask: Do descendants of such privilege owe anything to those whose blood, sweat, and lives built this country? Can you benefit from a system built on the backs of others and not be held responsible for its repair? Can you inherit privilege without paying the price for its pain?

Redemption isn't cheap. Recompense isn't either. Therefore, there can be no true redemption without recompense. And there is no justice without cost. If slavery lasted 250 years, then the healing must stretch at least twice as long. The debt doesn't disappear just because time passed. It compounds and we must reckon with that debt.

Throughout history, our culture—our music, our art, our resilience—has lulled America to sleep. Like David playing for Saul, we soothed the demons, and our rhythm pacified their guilt. But what happens when the music stops? What happens when the anointing behind the melody becomes clear? Once Saul saw David's anointing, the music became a threat.

America is afraid. Afraid of what could happen if the children of the enslaved were given a real seat at the table. Not a symbolic one—a real one and that seat must not only take up space but have an equal voice. It demands equal pay, equal protection, equal access, and equal power.

The whistle is still blowing. The steam is still rising. And the question God keeps asking this nation—and each of us—is the same:

Who's your daddy?

Are you still beholden to the father of lies, the architect of division, the one who built kingdoms on cruelty? Or have you come to know the Father of Light, the God of justice, the Defender of the oppressed? The days of pretending are over. The tea kettle has reached its limit. And so have we.

History has a heartbeat. And it doesn't just echo through time—it calls us to account.

It calls us to understand that the majority of the descendants of slaves do not carry purely African heritage. We are a melting pot of colors and races who make up the ethnic diversity, not just of this nation but also the confederacy. It was the blood, sweat, and tears of our ancestors that caused it to be a force to reckon with—not white slave owners. We are the ties that bind us together. And whether you like it or not, we are family.

As you consider the story of Hilliard and Emma, of love defying legacy, of conviction shattering custom, ask yourself: *What systems have I inherited? What silences have I kept? What injustices have I survived—or ignored?*

Knowing who you are is powerful, but knowing whose you are changes everything. We are not bound by the lies of supremacy, silence, or shame. We are heirs of a higher kingdom—one built on truth, justice, and unshakable love. The question isn't just who raised you, but who shaped you? What spirit fathered your worldview?

The whistle is still blowing. And it's not just calling out injustice—it's calling forth identity.

So, as the pressure builds and the sound rises, don't turn away. Don't reach for comfort. Lean in. Ask the question. Wrestle with the answer.

That steam does not lie; it is the voice of pressure speaking—pressure that has been building for generations, for centuries, in truth. That whistle is history trying to get your attention—trying to remind you that silence doesn't mean peace. And peace without truth? That's just anesthesia before the amputation.

Who's your daddy?

Because for many of us—descendants of slaves—that's not a simple answer. Daddy might've worn a crown in West Africa or he might've worn a whip on a plantation porch in Georgia. Some of our ancestors came in chains, and others came to claim. Our bloodlines are complicated—braided with pain, laced with contradiction. We don't just descend from kings and queens. We also descend from colonizers, rapists, and overseers.

We are not purely African, though Africa is our mother. Our skin tells stories the textbooks still don't have the courage to write. We are the blurred lines of race and resilience—the walking proof that America's hands were never clean.

Do you want to know who made the Confederacy a force to be reckoned with? It wasn't the men with mint juleps and muskets. It was the hands that harvested, the backs that bent, and the wombs that bore babies for sale.

It was **us**. It was the enslaved, the silenced, and the survivors. We didn't just build this country. We bled for it and that blood still speaks.

So go ahead and run the DNA tests. Check the census rolls. Search the family Bible you keep in the attic. Many white people who have been taught to hate Black people might be shocked to find that they have Black ancestors and relatives.

We are the ties that bind this house together—not them. We are the reckoning wrapped in a smile, and the justice that walks with grace. We are the broken branches of your family tree, still bearing fruit.

Who's your daddy?

And while you're at it—who are your people? Because ready or not... we're family.

Long before I knew anything about Hilliard and Emma—before I discovered their names on census records or uncovered the quiet rebellion of their love—I knew the sound of my mother's voice.

There's a strength in a mother's song that can carry generations. It soothes, yes, but it also teaches. It warns. It remembers.

The legacy of identity didn't begin with a whistle. It began with a melody. And that's where we turn next.

2

A MOTHER'S MELODY

When the world offered silence, she sang. When history
offered chains, she wove freedom into lullabies.

E si rose before the first bird broke the silence. The village slept beneath
a blanket of dreams, its stillness sacred, its breath held in the quiet reverence of dawn. Even the sea, restless and ancient, seemed to pause—its
waves hushed to a lull, as though listening for her footsteps. The thatched
roof above her head whispered with the wind, and through the open doorway, the soft stir of morning air carried the scent of saltwater, charcoal
smoke, and the damp sweetness of earth.

From the branches of the silk-cotton tree outside, birds began to call—
bright, high-pitched songs skipping from limb to limb. She hummed in
response, barely above a whisper, careful not to wake the others sleeping
on mats nearby. It was a soft melody, one she remembered from her childhood, shaped like a lullaby and heavy with memory. Then there was a stillness. The birds quieted as if they, too, were listening.

But inside, her thoughts churned like the tide. The day ahead pressed
in with quiet demands—fetching water from the stream, trading okra in
the market, avoiding the eyes of the men near the fort. *How will I man-*
age it all today?

She was pregnant and alone. Her husband had vanished months ago—first in silence, then in whispers. Some said he had fled inland, to avoid capture. Others claimed he had been taken—sold by a rival or betrayed by someone close. She had begged him to stay when the rumors began, clung to him with the desperation of someone trying to hold water in her hands. He had pulled away gently, then firmly, and finally, he was gone.

Now, she lived with her mother's cousin and her sons, in a home not her own, among people who watched her belly grow but spoke little of what was to come. She helped where she could, kept her voice soft, her back straight, and her eyes low. But she was not like the other women who accepted their place. She would not settle. Her spirit refused to yield, not then, and not even now.

She had no clear plan, no midwife yet chosen, and no name for the child she carried. But she knew. She knew in the aching silence between the waves, in the long, unspoken stares of the elders, and in her dreams filled with fire and flight, that this child was not ordinary.

She was pregnant with a nation. One she might never see. One that might be dragged screaming through the Door of No Return, or born to run barefoot through fields she would never know.

Still, it kicked. Still, it stirred. And so, she rose—to sing, to carry, to endure.

She wrapped her cloth tight around her waist and slipped out with a calabash balanced neatly atop her head. She moved with the grace of one who knew the world before words—before the taking, before the wailing, before the names were lost. Her hands, dark as the soil and worn smoothly by work, pressed gently against her belly. There, in the sacred curve of her body, a life moved. Not just a child, but a promise, a future, a lament, and a legacy.

This was not the first morning she had risen before the sun. But today felt different—hollowed out by a silence that reached beyond sleep. Something in the air trembled. The spirits in the trees did not stir. The drums were silent. Even the sky seemed unsure whether to weep or to wait.

She stepped to the threshold of her home, bare feet meeting the cool earth. The land beneath her had known centuries of joy and sorrow, harvest and hunger, blood and birth. But today, it felt like goodbye.

And though her lips did not part, though her voice made no sound, there was music in her movement. It was a melody rising from within— a song only the ancestors could hear. It was the sound of generations wrapped in her womb. A mother's cry tucked beneath her breath. A lullaby laced with grief and unspoken knowing.

The morning sun had not yet cleared the treetops, and the narrow path toward the market was still shaded and cool. Around her, the village stirred to life—a cough here, a rooster's call there, and the rhythmic sound of a pestle crushing yam into fufu. Life, as it was known, continued. But something in her spirit tugged sideways.

She reached the fork in the footpath, where one trail led inland toward the chatter of trade and the other curved east, through a wild bush, toward the sea cliffs. Her feet, without asking, chose the latter. She had not climbed the cliffs in many moons—not since the swelling of her belly had turned balance into a quiet risk. But today, something stirred within her. Something unseen pulled her upward, as if the wind itself remembered her name.

The higher she climbed, the quieter it became. Only the wind remained, brushing past her ears like a spirit whispering a secret.

When she reached the ridge, the sea spread before her like an endless sheet of hammered metal—bright, vast, and trembling. Below, waves slapped angrily at the rocks. She placed the calabash down beside her and sat.

And then she saw it. Far off, yet undeniable—was a ship. It was not a canoe or fishing vessel. This one was larger and darker. Its sails folded like wings. It moved slowly and deliberately, like a predator stalking its prey.

It was a slave ship. One of the many that came not with the rhythm of trade, but with the silence of capture.

She had seen them in the past—their arrival whispered through the village long before the mast crested the horizon. The men near the fort would grow busy. The markets would grow quiet. And someone—always someone—would be missing the next day.

But this time was different. She had *watched* it arrive. Her hand moved instinctively to her belly. The baby inside kicked once, then again—sharp and certain.

She squinted, heart clenching, and watching small black dots move on the sand below, near the base of the fort. Men were unloading crates. Others were preparing for the procession. She could not see their faces, but she knew the feeling in the air. It was the same feeling she had the night her husband disappeared—the press of something approaching and heavy with finality.

This was not a day for the market. This was a day for remembering. She did not know whether she would return to the path or whether she would descend. For a long moment, she just sat, watching the ship slide closer, like a blade slipping into flesh. And beneath her ribs, the child turned—not in fear but in knowing.

She stayed until the ship's hull kissed the edge of the bay and its anchor rattled into the sea with a low, grinding groan. Below her, figures moved like ants—some local, some foreign—men in cloth and men in coats, all walking in lines that meant nothing good.

Still, she did not move. Her lips pressed shut, her breath slow and shallow, as though she feared the wind might carry her presence down to the men who sold flesh and called it profit.

It was only when the first cries floated up—faint, but unmistakable—did she rise. They were not market cries. They weren't fish cries. They were human cries. The kind pulled from the throat, not the tongue.

She bent to pick up her calabash, though she had long since forgotten what she meant to trade. Her fingers trembled slightly, the way they had the night she found his sandals gone from the doorway. The night she lay awake, her belly still flat and her body still hopeful.

He had said nothing. He gave no farewell. He only left behind the sound of a door closing and a quiet she would never forgive.

Her feet began to move faster now. She turned back toward the village, leaving the market path behind as if it had never been her destination. The cliffs had shown her what she needed to see—not just the ship, but what it meant—that nothing would wait. It revealed that safety was a story, and silence was a weapon.

As she descended the ridge, she saw her cousin's son crouched by the cassava patch, looking up at the same dark ship she had watched. He was only ten, but he had the eyes of someone who'd learned too much too early. When he saw her, he didn't wave—he just nodded, like an old man. She nodded back, and they said nothing.

Back in the village, women prepared cassava, dried peppers, and scrubbed pots, but their hands moved slower than usual. There was no laughter and no gossip. There was only the occasional glance toward the direction of the fort.

And there, standing at the edge of the path like a post struck in the earth, was Adjoa—old, wrapped in rust-colored cloth, and eyes sharp as flint.

"I saw you go," Adjoa said without greeting. "You climbed."

She nodded.

"You saw it then."

Again, she nodded.

Adjoa's eyes shifted to the curve of her belly. "The child comes at a time of blood."

"I know."

"You carry more than a child, girl."

"I know."

They stood there in the quiet, women who had seen too much and not enough.

"Don't go to the market today," Adjoa said. "They will be watching. Choosing."

"I wasn't going to."

Adjoa stepped aside. "Come. We'll burn leaves—make smoke. We'll make them think we are mourning someone already gone."

She followed. And as they walked, she felt the baby inside shift again—not in fear, but readiness. The kind that comes before a storm or a birth.

By midday, a haze had begun to settle over the village. There was a thin curtain of smoke rising from pots of bitter leaves and charred orange peels. The elders said it kept sickness away. But today, it served another purpose.

It was mourning smoke. It was a message and a warning.

Women walked slowly between homes with bowls of herbs and salt, heads covered, and mouths tight. Children were kept indoors. Even the chickens clucked quieter than usual.

The men from the fort were watching—waiting for the right moment to seize more bodies. They came before the rain, when the earth was soft enough to swallow resistance. The ship's captain claimed they had reached their quota at the last full moon, but everyone knew the truth: for the traders, there was no such thing as enough. The Europeans called them "cargo," as if human souls could be stacked and stored like sacks of dried beans.

Adjoa and the other elder women gathered near the firepit in the center of the compound. They did not sit. They stirred. They moved in and out of shadow, speaking in proverbs and glances, in names half-spoken and paths not taken.

She stayed close by, grinding dried okra into powder while keeping an ear open. Her belly had grown heavier in the past weeks, shifting her balance and pace. But she listened well.

"They took Kojo's cousin at the river last market day," Adjoa said quietly, not looking up. "He was just fetching water. No chains, just silence. Gone."

A low murmur followed.

"They'll be at the market by morning. Looking for bodies. Strong backs. Empty ties."

"We must hide the boys," another woman said.

"Not just boys. They're taking girls now too."

Her grip tightened on the pestle. A sharp ache pulsed in her lower back. The child kicked, almost in agreement.

Then came the soft shuffling of feet. A young boy, maybe twelve, appeared behind the women—narrow-faced, breathless. "They're coming," he whispered. "A white man with a list. He's from the ship."

The circle broke into motion. Women left the fire without a word, peeling away like bark, each one disappearing into her assigned role. Some would distract. Others would hide. One would wail loud enough to confuse.

Adjoa turned to her. "Go to Amma's hut. The one with the broken calabash above the door. Stay low. She knows what to do."

She nodded, rose slowly, and made her way through the narrow footpaths. Every step felt weighted—not just by the child, but by history, by fear, and by some unspoken vow she had never agreed to but now carried.

As she passed a house, she saw a father slip his son into the ground—a false cellar carved out beneath a mat. Two boys vanished into clay like seeds.

The fort men were close now. Voices echoed, boots against earth. A dog barked once, then went silent.

She ducked behind a woven fence. Her heart hammering. Through the gaps, she saw them. A tall white man in a blue coat, sweating under the sun, his boots too clean for the land. Beside him, a local man—younger, bare-chested, holding a list.

They were not choosing bodies. They were choosing futures to erase. The child inside her shifted again. It was no longer a flutter. It was a warning—a vow.

The hut sat low and crooked at the far end of the compound, half-swallowed by banana leaves and shadows. Its thatched roof sagged with age, and the clay walls bore the color of dried blood. Above the door, tied with a frayed strip of palm, hung a broken calabash. Its cracked mouth tilted to the side like it had once tried to speak and failed.

She ducked inside quickly, drawing the reed door closed behind her. The air was thick and dry, filled with the smell of old wood smoke, dried herbs, and something else—older and bitter. Like roots dug too deep.

The room was dim, lit only by narrow shafts of light slipping through the wall slats. Her eyes adjusted slowly. There were no windows, only the soft huddle of objects pressed against the walls: jars sealed with wax, bowls of powdered chalk, and bundles of leaves suspended from the rafters.

In the center, seated cross-legged, was Amma. She was small—not in frame, but in presence—like someone who had folded herself in half too many times to fit inside other people's rules. Her hair was wrapped in indigo cloth; her arms covered in the pale dust of ground baobab bark. Her eyes lifted slowly to meet the younger woman's.

"You've come," Amma said, as though it had been foretold.

"They said—Adjoa said—"

Amma raised a hand. "Sit."

She sat, resting against the cool earth, grateful to be off her feet. There was silence between them for a moment—not the kind that waited to be broken, but the kind that held something.

Then Amma leaned forward and reached for a gourd. She poured thick liquid into a small wooden cup and handed it over. "Drink."

"What is it?"

"Something bitter. But it clears the path."

She hesitated, then drank. It tasted of smoke and root, with the sting of something unripe. Her eyes watered.

Amma nodded, approving.

"You carry a child born of breaking," Amma said. "A child that knows things before they're told."

She blinked, startled. "How do you—?"

"There are only a few born like that each generation. When the world is about to turn over. They come through women whose backs are strong enough to carry silence without folding."

A beat passed.

"They are always born near the sea," Amma added. She felt the baby shift again—not like a kick this time, but a stretch, a push toward something. Her throat tightened.

Outside, the footsteps passed closer—men calling out names in broken Fante, dogs sniffing at footprints, and then the sudden high-pitched wailing of a woman down the path. It was a performance—a delay. Amma did not flinch.

"These men will not stop," she said. "But you must. For a while. The child must not be born into their gaze. It must come clean, under moonlight, far from the fort."

Tears pricked her eyes, not from fear but from the ache of being seen—truly seen. Her whole life had been a kind of hiding. Now it had a name—a purpose.

"You are not just carrying a child," Amma whispered. "You are carrying memory—a kind that will try to survive even when the language is beaten from the tongue and the names are stolen. That's what they fear the most."

The door rustled. Her breath caught. But it was only a hand—Adjoa's—sliding through a small opening in the side wall.

"They've passed," she whispered. "You're safe. For now."

Amma stood. "Go. But come back before the next moon. There is more you must learn." She nodded, slowly rising.

Outside, the air felt heavier. It wasn't heavy with fear, but with weight. It carried the feeling of knowing, as if the earth itself understood what was coming. She left the hut with one hand on her belly, and the other brushing the broken calabash as she passed. It was not broken, she now realized. It had simply poured out what it had to give.

The moon had returned, round and swollen like her belly—a silver twin floating above the canopy, casting its light not with brilliance, but with quiet insistence. It was the kind of moon that listened more than it shone.

She moved through the bush paths just before midnight, her feet brushing against dew-soaked leaves. Every step felt heavier and the child within her restless, as though sensing that the world was preparing for something.

She wore no bells, no color, only a deep wrap of dyed indigo and a strip of leather tied around her wrist—a charm Amma had given her. "For strength, not safety," she had said. "You must choose your danger."

The village had grown quieter over the past weeks, though tension lingered like woodsmoke in the rafters. Rumors whispered of more ships arriving, of boys disappearing in the night, of a girl who vanished on her way to the river and was never found. But no one spoke these things aloud. They were folded into work songs, pounded into yam, and carried in the way women glanced behind them before crossing thresholds.

She reached the hut with the broken calabash and found the door ajar, the glow of coal casting a dull red heartbeat inside. Amma was waiting, just as before—only this time, she wasn't alone.

Another woman sat beside her. She was older, wrapped in a shawl of coarse linen, her eyes sharp and unblinking. Between them sat a wide, shallow bowl filled with water so still it looked like polished stone.

"Come," Amma said, gesturing to the place between them. She sat. Her bones ached from the walk, and her stomach pulled tight with quiet waves of discomfort. The child shifted again—more deliberate now. It was no longer a flutter but a signal.

Amma's voice was low. "This is Nana Eshe. She was there when the last one came through. It was before the droughts and before the new governor built the eastern wall. She has waited many years to see this again."

Nana Eshe nodded once, then placed her palm gently on the younger woman's wrist. Her skin was like tree bark—rough, wise, and living.

"You carry one who remembers before they are born," she said, in a voice deep with age and earth. "This is not new. It only feels new because forgetting has become a custom."

They leaned over the bowl. Amma dropped in a sprig of dried mint and a pinch of ash. Then, slowly, she placed in the bowl a stone wrapped in a strip of cloth. The water trembled. Images swam in it—faint and broken, like shadows behind mist.

She saw flashes of shorelines. There were chains being buried. Someone had a hand raised. She noticed a child with her eyes but a face she didn't recognize, standing on land where the trees grew differently. They spoke in a tongue that bent around English like roots around stone.

She gasped. Amma steadied her.

"It is not prophecy," she said. "It is remembering forward."

"What does that mean?"

Nana Eshe spoke. "It means the child you carry may never know this place, but they will know *you*. They will feel your hands, your song, and your blood. Even when they are taken, your memory goes with them."

A long silence passed. Then Amma's voice again: "You must give birth away from here. Not near the market, not near the forts. When the pains come, follow the northern trail to the black tree near the river bend. We will meet you there." She nodded, her throat too tight for words.

"Your name will be carried," Amma whispered. "Not by scroll. Not by stone. But by breath." Outside, a breeze passed through the trees, carrying with it the smell of the sea—salt, iron, and distance.

She looked at the bowl again, but the water had gone still. Her future had not disappeared. It had only hidden itself in her child.

The heat came early that morning—thick, pressing, like a warning dressed as weather. The birds did not sing. The goats bleated low and unsettled. Even the children, usually loud with sunrise, moved quietly between huts, their games abandoned, and their laughter swallowed.

She did not know that this would be the last dawn she'd ever see in her homeland. That the sea, now calm, would soon swallow her screams. That the child she carried would be born in chains beneath a foreign sun.

She felt it before she saw it—that slow, unnatural hush that fell across the village like the shadow of something vast. *The traders had returned.*

She was pounding cassava with the elder women, though her belly made the task slower. She hadn't told anyone that the pain had started the night before, faint and low like distant drums. There was no time to honor her body—not now. Not when the sails were visible again on the horizon. Three ships approached, each bearing foreign flags. Their hulls heavy with emptiness and waiting to be filled.

"They are early," muttered one of the women beside her, never pausing the rhythm of her pestle.

"No," said another. "They are *hungry*."

A messenger from the nearby outpost—a boy barely old enough to hold a knife, with a tunic too large and eyes rimmed red from dust. "They've come for more," he said. "I heard the fort master say five bodies. Young and strong."

She staggered back to her hut, heart pounding harder than the child inside her. The vision from the bowl returned like fever—the shadowed face of her unborn, the strange lands, and the tongue that bent like smoke. But now, another image intruded: a rope, a neck, and a name forgotten in the wind. She sat down hard, the pressure in her belly mounting. Adjoa found her moments later.

"They are choosing names already," she whispered. "They've written yours."

She blinked. "Mine?"

"You are not married. You do not own land. You do not belong to any elder's household. You are—"

"Expendable."

Adjoa flinched but didn't deny it. Her mouth went dry. Her hands trembled. Now, the choice had to be made. She could run—follow the northern trail Amma spoke of, past the black tree, to the secret bend in the river. The birth would come there, clean and hidden.

She could stay—plead with the chief, offer herself up as a healer, as a teacher of children, or as *anything*. Or she could fight—not with blade or fire, but with what Amma called *memory*. The kind of memory that hides inside names, songs, and resistance whispered in the dark.

The sky outside was turning gold at the edges. She had until nightfall. She placed her hand on her belly. The child shifted—not in fear, but in readiness.

Then, quietly, she spoke: "I will not go bound." She rose—not to run or beg, but to gather herself. She needed strength for what lay ahead.

She first sought out Adjoa, then the young men who still remembered the drum signals of the old language. Next, she found the midwife who once stitched a wound without shedding a tear, and finally the boy who climbed trees taller than the palm watchtowers.

If they would take her name, she would make sure it meant something. If they would come for her child, they would find not a woman, but a nation already waking.

The moon was a sliver this time—sharp as a blade, half-hidden behind clouds that moved too quickly. The wind had changed. It no longer smelled of rain or ripe mangoes. It carried salt, tar, and iron.

She had not made it to the river. They had come sooner than she planned—with torches and guns, with names already written and debts counted. It wasn't the governor's soldiers who found her. It was the middlemen. They were the ones who spoke her language. Those who wore her skin. The ones who knew where to look.

She had almost made it to the bend—so close—when a sudden flash of firelight caught her from the side. She ran, fast and barefoot, her belly low to the ground, and her breath breaking into sobs. But they were faster and younger. They carried no burden. They tackled her beneath a tamarind tree. The same tree where she once played as a child. "No harm to the belly," one of them warned, breathless.

They looped a rope around her wrists. Another man bound her ankles. She fought—not with screams, but with silence so full of fury it rattled the leaves above them.

"You don't understand," she whispered. But they did. That was the worst part. They understood. And still, they did it.

She was brought back at dawn through the village, barefoot and bleeding. Her dress was torn and her hair was matted with soil and sweat. People turned away. Some cried. Others could not look. The chief did not speak.

She was placed in the square with the others—four boys, one girl barely old enough to be called that. They had tried to hide too. All of them were bound at the wrists, backs straight, eyes searching.

The traders stood at a distance, flanked by armed guards, their foreign tongues slicing through the humid air like axes. One of them pointed to her belly and raised a brow. The chief gave a slow nod. The trader laughed. "Double price," someone muttered.

She looked at the crowd and found Adjoa, standing near the cooking huts, tears on her cheeks. Behind her, in the shadows, stood Amma—unflinching. She watched, raised one hand to her chest and tapped it once.

Remember.

They were marched to the coast by midday, the sun high and merciless. Her ankles blistered. Her wrists ached. Her baby kicked once. Then it kicked again. The child was still there—still waiting.

They passed the path she would've taken—the one that led to the river, to the black tree, to the place where she had hoped to give birth in secret and silence. That path remained untouched for now.

At the cliffside, the ship loomed—black wood, with sails like wings folded in judgment. Smoke curled from its belly.

They lined the captives in rows. They inspected them like livestock. They poked and prodded.

When they reached her, she did not lower her gaze. She stared straight into the eyes of the man who opened her mouth, checked her teeth, and touched her stomach like it was a parcel to be weighed.

"She is too far along," one trader said in Portuguese. "Then take her now," another answered. "Before the child comes."

She was pulled toward the ramp, her feet dragging. And still, in her mind, a song began to form—one she had not yet sung aloud. It was a song meant for someone far away. It was for someone not yet born but who would not forget.

They called it *The Deliverance*—though no deliverance waited within. The hull of the ship groaned like an old beast, heavy with bodies and iron. The moment she crossed the gangplank, something inside her slipped— not the child, not yet—but something in her soul that once believed in mercy. It cracked, quietly, like a small bone in winter.

The stench hit first: sweat, feces, vomit, salt, and sorrow—layered thick over the wood like old lacquer. She was shoved below deck, past screaming men, wailing women, and people who were already too broken to make a sound.

They chained her to a row of women—all wide-eyed, some still bleeding from where their earrings had been ripped away. A bucket in the corner overflowed. A baby cried until it didn't. Somewhere nearby, someone sang under their breath, the notes barely louder than breathing. No one knew each other's names. No one asked.

That night—or what she guessed was night, for there was no light save for the cracks in the boards above—her child shifted again. Her body ached. She bit the inside of her cheek to keep from groaning. Beside her, a woman whose leg had been shattered during the march whispered something. It sounded like a prayer. Or maybe it was a memory.

"I left my daughter in the yam fields…"

The ship lurched, and they all moved with it, like sacks of grain lashed together. Rats scurried in the corners. A crewman opened the hatch once to toss down what passed for food, but no one reached for it—not yet.

They learned quickly: Don't cry out. Don't resist. Don't catch the eye of the ones who come with torches. They take the ones who scream.

Still, she watched. Every hour, she counted the sounds above—the boots, the chains, and the clicks of metal. She studied the boards and how they flexed. She marked which guards drank too much, which ones spat when they walked, and which one had the limp.

She was not just *observing*. She was *surviving*. On the third day—or maybe the fourth—they brought her topside for air. She squinted at the sky, too bright, and too blue. The ocean stretched endlessly in all directions, mocking her memory of land. She remembered her hut, the face of Amma, and the river trail she had not reached. But the sky also held clouds that moved like birds, like directions, and like omens.

She was forced to wash herself in a bucket while men watched. Her belly had dropped. She would not have weeks. Maybe not even days.

A sailor noticed. He spoke to the captain in clipped Dutch. She didn't know the words, but she knew the tone. They didn't want her to give birth on the ship. It was too messy, too dangerous, and far too human.

That night, she was briefly unchained while the crew argued over her fate. It was a mercy—and a mistake. She used the moment to whisper to the woman beside her. Just a name. Just a breath.

"Esi," she said. The woman blinked. Then whispered her own: "Ama."

They shared no more. But that was enough. It had begun. A remembering had stirred. A weaving had quietly taken shape.

In the dark belly of *The Deliverance*, with iron biting skin and hope hanging by a thread, they passed names—small, precious things. A village. A song. A story. A warning. Passed from mouth to mouth like stolen fire.

They could take her body. They would not take her memory. And when her child began to come—in pain, in silence, and in salt-slick agony— she did not scream.

She sang. It was a song the ocean would not understand but would never forget. It began in the stillest part of night—when even the rats had gone quiet and the crew above staggered drunk under the stars. Her water broke without warning, soaking the filthy planks beneath her, merging with blood and brine already baked into the wood. A few around her stirred, eyes wide in the dark.

She pressed her back to the hull, teeth gritted. A sharpness tore through her belly. There was no midwife, no herbs, and no warm cloths. There was just iron on her ankles, a single hand to squeeze—Ama's—and the breath of other captives holding vigil around her.

"Push, sister," one whispered. She obeyed—silent, teeth clenched, pushing against the weight of the world, against the chains that held her, and against the memory that refused to let go. Her cry was the sound of thunder trapped in a cave. Her sweat rolled like rivers, and still she pushed.

The ship creaked with the rhythm of labor. Her body folded forward when another contraction came. Her voice—at last—escaped her throat, guttural and low. She wasn't sure if it was a song or a scream. Maybe it was both. And then—in the half-dark, beneath the stench and sorrow— a small cry pierced the air. It was high, fragile, and alive.

The other women turned toward her, their eyes glinting in the shadows—sharp with approval, soft with wonder. A gasp escaped from one, followed by the trembling sound of a weeping laugh, the kind that carries both grief and relief in a single breath. Someone began humming—that same half-song she'd heard before. It wove through the hold like smoke.

The child was slick, brown, and wailing. A girl. Tiny fists curled. Eyes shut. But lungs strong.

Ama bit the umbilical cord and tied it with a strip torn from her own tunic. They wrapped the child in what they had—a scrap of cloth, still damp, still enough.

She cradled the baby to her chest, trembling. Her name came like a whisper from some place older than language. *"Afi..."* Meaning, *"Born on a Friday."*

The ship above remained unaware. But something had shifted below. She was not the only one who felt it. The others leaned close, drawing near, not to stare but to shield—to make their bodies into a wall, a cradle of limbs and warmth. In that circle, for one breathless moment, she was not a captive. She was a mother. She was a woman surrounded by kin. But morning would come soon. And they would find out. The sea did not hush for the birth of the child, but it remembered her.

Long after the cries faded and the captain's curses settled into the planks, long after the mother's blood dried in the grooves of the deck, the ocean still carried the sound—tucked deep beneath the waves, where only the old things listen.

They did not name the child on the manifest. No ledger recorded her arrival. She was not cargo, or crew. She was something else—something the ship feared, and the sea understood.

The crew debated her fate in harsh tongues. Some said she was a curse, born of fetters and silence. Others saw her as a sign—an omen that they had trespassed too far, that the very waters beneath them had grown restless. The mother, bruised but unbowed, whispered her daughter's name only to the waves.

"Afi."

They let her keep the child, perhaps out of pity, or superstition, or a fear they would not name. But they began to avoid her in the lower hold, where she sat nursing by candle stub, rocking as the ship rocked, humming lullabies born of rivers, fires, and things that once had names.

She told Afi stories with no end. She told stories of forests so green they hummed, of drums that called ancestors' home, of women who could speak with birds, and of a village where the moon dipped low enough to touch the crown of a newborn's head.

Afi never cried again—not once. The other captives began to say she was not of this world. That she had come through her mother, yes, but from someplace older. They believed that she would not die, settle, or serve. She would drift always—untethered—across waters that called her name.

And one night, just past the halfway mark of the voyage, when the moon was too full and the wind too still, the ship rocked in a sudden silence. And in the morning—the mother was there but the child *was not*. There was no splash heard. There were no remains—only the salt dried on her skin and the hush that followed. The captain said nothing. He had seen things, once, on another voyage. He did not wish to see them again.

But still, she stood. Still, she listened. Still, she sang. For even as the world ripped her from the only soil she'd ever known, her soul held fast to the melody. The one every mother carries. The one that births nations. But the mother, staring out at the place where the sea met the sky, said only this: *"She does not belong to land. She belongs to the water that bore her."*

And the others—still chained, still caged—believed her. They, too, had heard the sea singing that night. It was not cruel and not cold—but calling. Somewhere, perhaps in the belly of a wave or hidden in the memory of rain, a girl named Afi still listens. She still floats. She still waits—not for rescue, but for remembering.

"A Motherland Melody"

I heard her voice in the wind last night,
Whispers of rivers and red-gold light.
A lullaby through the broken trees,
Calling me home on the ocean's breeze.

She wore the sun in her braided hair,
Danced in the dust like she was still there.
But they tore me from her arms so wide—
Now, I'm just echoes on the tide.

[Chorus]
Oh, Motherland, can you feel my cry?
I was born in chains, but I dream in sky.
Your heartbeat drums through this foreign sand,
I'm still your child… oh, Motherland.

[Verse 2]
They sold our names, and they broke our songs,
Told us forgetting would make us strong.
But I still see your smile in flames,
Still feel your blood running through my veins.

I carry stories I've never told,
Languages carved into ancient soul.
Though I walk roads you'll never see,
Your spirit walks right next to me.

[Chorus]
Oh, Motherland, can you feel my cry?
I was born in chains, but I dream in sky.
Your heartbeat drums through this foreign sand,
I'm still your child… oh, Motherland.

[Bridge]

This love is pain, this love is pride,

The tears of oceans we could not hide.

But through the sorrow, through the flame,

I rise in you, I speak your name.

[Outro]

So when I sing to the stars above,

Know every note is a rebel's love.

One day, my feet will touch your land,

And you will hold me... Motherland.

Before I ever traced a bloodline or read a name on a fragile census paper, I heard the song of my mother. It was not just in lyrics you'd find in a hymnal, but in the way she *lived*—each movement a note, each breath a chord strung tight between grief and grit. Her voice didn't echo through microphones or grand stages. It moved softer than that—like wind weaving through trees, like water whispering over stones. You had to listen close. You had to listen with your soul.

She didn't just sing lullabies to soothe us into dreams either. She sang *truths*—to keep us from sleeping through our own becoming. Her melody was the first sound I ever knew, and somehow, I still carry it—deep in the marrow of my bones.

There was music in the mundane: In the scrape of the wooden spoon against a cast iron pot. It was in the hush of her hums as she braided a crown of plaits on weary heads, and in the prayers that tiptoed through cracked doorways, cloaked in hush, and wrapped in hope. Her melody didn't rise for applause—it rose to survive and overcome.

That was her gift: a song too sacred for sheet music. It was an inheritance not etched in wills or wealth but carried in bone and spirit. She passed down no dowries—but she gave us a sound that couldn't be silenced.

It was a legacy with very little land, yet more fertile than any field—a legacy of wisdom, memory, and the will to keep going.

She taught me how to listen between the lines—between what was said and what was suffered. She showed me that memory has music. That if you're still enough, and if you surrender to silence, you'll hear the hum of history—the heartbeat of those who came before. Still singing. Still teaching. Still surviving through us.

This is not just her story. It's the chorus of every mother who bore nations in the shadows. It was the song of every woman who bore the weight of a world that refused to carry her. The hymn of women who stitched broken dreams into blankets and covered generations. The song of Black mothers who rocked babies with one arm while holding up collapsing worlds with the other.

It is the music of survival. The sound that made me. The sound that *made us all.*

What songs live in your bones? What whispers echo in your quiet moments—long after the voices are gone, long after the names have faded from paper and memory?

We are shaped by the melodies we inherit, even when we don't know the lyrics. The rhythm of resilience, the harmony of hope, and the dissonance of survival—all of it lives in us. And perhaps the greatest honor we can give to those who came before is to keep singing. We must speak not just with our mouths, but with our lives—drawing truth from deep within our souls.

Listen. What is the melody of our Mother land calling you to remember and to become? But even the strongest songs sometimes fade. Even the sweetest melody can be carried off—Gone with the Wind.

3

GONE WITH
THE WIND

What history tried to divide, blood has already bound.

The wind whispered through the towering oaks, ancient sentinels watching over Letohatchee, Alabama. Their gnarled branches swayed and groaned, bearing witness to centuries of silence, secrets, and sin. Beneath them, the plantation stretched wide and far, a kingdom built on the backs of the broken. Hilliard stood on the porch of his father's house, staring across the land that had raised him—land that no longer felt like his.

He inhaled deeply, letting the warm, cotton-scented air fill his lungs. The soil beneath his feet had once felt sacred. Now, it felt cursed. Every row of cotton whispered of pain. Every gust of wind carried the voices of the enslaved—crying and singing to survive. His eyes drifted to the barn, where a lone figure moved beneath the amber light of the sinking sun.

Emma. She moved with the grace of someone who had learned how to be invisible in plain sight. Her hands were busy, threading needle through sack, but even from this distance, Hilliard could feel the pull of her presence. She had always been different—sunlight wrapped in skin, soft-spoken but fierce in spirit. He could still hear her laughter from years ago, echoing through the kitchens, through the fields, through the corners of his heart.

What are you doing, Hilliard? he thought. *What do you think you're going to say that could make this right?*

He stepped off the porch, boots crunching against the dry earth. Every step felt heavy, like the weight of generations was pressing down on his shoulders. He had returned from Raleigh only weeks ago, but it felt like a lifetime. He thought he was just coming home. Instead, he had walked into a battlefield.

Emma looked up as he neared, her hands stilling. Her dark eyes met his, calm and unreadable. She didn't flinch, didn't smile. There was only that look—steady like the land.

"Good evening, Miss Emma," he said, his voice more clipped than he meant.

A faint smile curved her lips, though sorrow lived in it. "Good evening, Master Hilliard."

The title twisted in his gut. "You don't have to call me that."

"I do," she said simply, returning her eyes to her hands. "We both know why."

He stood silent for a moment, watching her fingers move like water, patching broken things with quiet skill. "You were always good with your hands," he murmured.

"I do what I'm told."

"That's not what I meant."

Emma looked up again, her eyes now clouded with something he couldn't name. "Then what did you mean?"

He hesitated. How do you confess a love that has no right to exist? How do you speak truth in a world built on lies?

"I meant... you could do anything. Be anything."

Her hands stilled. The sack lay forgotten in her lap. "You sound like a man who doesn't know what chains are."

He stepped closer. "Maybe I'm just now learning."

She shook her head. "You don't learn by looking at me like that. You learn by seeing what I see."

"And what do you see?" he asked, voice barely a whisper.

Emma's gaze didn't falter. "I see a man torn in two. I see a world that will burn you down for even standing here with me. I see danger in your eyes—not because you want to hurt me, but because you don't understand what your love will cost."

He wanted to argue, to protest, and to say that love was worth it. But the truth was that he didn't fully understand—not yet.

And yet... "I want to try."

Silence fell. The wind picked up, rustling the trees, the cotton, and the ghosts. Emma stood. "Wanting isn't enough, Hilliard. They wanted to hang my uncle for looking at a white girl too long. They beat my cousin for speaking too loudly. Your wanting doesn't protect me."

His hands balled into fists at his sides. "Then what do I do?"

She walked past him, toward the barn doors, then paused. "You tell me when you're ready to burn it all down. The house. The name. The inheritance. The illusion." She disappeared into the shadows, leaving Hilliard alone with the wind and his choices.

The wind died down as the barn door creaked shut behind her, and Hilliard was left in a silence more deafening than thunder. He stared into the shadows, searching for her outline, but Emma had vanished. Just like she always did when he stepped too close.

He turned back toward the house, shoulders heavy with words unsaid. As he walked up the steps and pushed through the grand doors, memories flooded him—laughter echoing in the dining room, polished silverware glinting under chandelier light, and his father's voice booming from the study.

His mother was there, seated by the window, stitching lace into one of her handkerchiefs. She looked up, and her expression soured the moment she saw him.

"You've been out there again," she said flatly.

"I was walking the grounds."

She narrowed her eyes. "With her."

"Her name is Emma."

"I don't care what her name is," his mother snapped, her needle stabbing the fabric with force. "She is not one of us."

"She's not property either."

"You sound like your father when he drank too much whiskey and whispered about his regrets. Don't make the same mistakes."

Hilliard sat across from her, jaw clenched. "He never acknowledged what he did. He never claimed the children he fathered. Do you know what that did to them? To her?"

His mother's hand froze. "This house was built to last. Don't be the one to bring it down." But it was already falling, he thought. Crumbling beneath the weight of its own sins.

That night, sleep eluded him. He lay in bed staring at the ceiling, the creak of the old house sounding like whispered warnings. He thought of Emma—her strength, her sorrow, and the chain she wore not on her wrists but in her silence. He dreamt of their childhood—of him sneaking biscuits from the kitchen to share with her under the sycamore tree. He thought of her laughter and of the day she stopped laughing.

When morning came, Hilliard rose with fire in his chest. The town would be at church that Sunday. He knew what he had to do.

The congregation filled the pews of the whitewashed chapel, their voices rising in hymns that praised a God they didn't fully understand. Hilliard stood from his family's designated row, walked to the front, and turned to face them.

"I have something to say," he announced. Heads turned. His mother's face went pale.

"I am marrying Emma." Gasps rippled through the sanctuary. The pastor froze mid-verse. His mother stood in protest.

"She is a woman of dignity, strength, and more honor than half the men in this room. If that means I lose my name, my inheritance, or this house, then let it all burn. I choose her."

The silence was violent. When he exited the church, stones were hurled— not all literal, but every insult, every slur, every glare cut deep.

Listen. Can you hear their assaults disguised as insults being hurled at him? Can you feel the onslaught of the hatred he endured? By sundown, his name was poison. His mother closed the doors of the house to him. Merchants refused him service. Neighbors turned away.

But Emma opened her door. He stood on her doorstep, bruised by the hatred of a town he once called home. She looked at him, no words spoken—only eyes that had seen too much, and a heart that had waited too long.

And finally, he stepped forward, not as a master, but as a man shedding his skin, unlearning power, and walking into the fire for love. Because that's what love does. It burns illusions to the ground. It remakes a man. It sets two souls free.[2]

---

2. This chapter presents a fictitious reenactment of the events that could've taken place between my ancestors, Hilliard and Emma, based on the factual accounts I found on Ancestry.com (Please see Figures pages).

4

GOD'S LOVE SONG

*"Stand at the crossroads and look; ask for the ancient
paths, ask where the good way is, and walk in
it, and you will find rest for your souls."*

JEREMIAH 6:16, NIV

S ome songs are written in silence—before the first breath, before the first heartbreak. There are some that existed before chains, before choices, even before memory.

Mine began with love—not fleeting or fairytale, but fierce and consecrated. The kind that teaches a daughter to love God by watching her father worship Him. My father was my first safe place, my first rhythm. He taught me how to pray without uttering a word, how to weep without shame, and how to trust God when the music stopped.

I didn't know it then, but I was being taught to recognize God's love songs—the kind that aren't sung with lips, but with lives.

I think of Hilliard and Emma now. How their love, like mine, was never *supposed* to be possible. Not by law. Not by custom. Not by the crooked code of a country bound by blood and blinded by its own design.

A white son of a Southern plantation. A Black woman born in bondage. They should've been a footnote. A warning. A scandal. But instead, they became a verse in God's redemptive refrain—a melody that echoed through time and landed softly in the folds of my own story. Their love was a protest. A praise. A prophecy. And so was mine.

I was nearly sixteen when my father—my melody—had a stroke. The song of my childhood skipped, cracked, and eventually fell silent when he passed. With his death, the foundation I had stood on crumbled beneath me. I staggered. I searched for the music again, desperate to hear anything that sounded like love.

Instead, I walked into noise. I ended up in a marriage at nineteen—violent, chaotic, and soul-crushing. Three times death reached for me through the hands of the man I trusted, and three times God intervened. *He will not let your foot slip. He who watches over you does not sleep.*[3]

Out of the ashes of that wreckage came my son—a warrior born from war. His service, his sacrifice, and his survival all sang a different tune. And still, God was composing.

Seven years later, I married again. This time, the notes were softer. We laughed, raised children, and dreamed. But time has a way of re-arranging songs, and after 23 years, our duet faded into dissonance. I wept, not because it ended—but because God whispered that it wasn't over.

Yes, I heard Him—as clearly as the wind that brushed Emma's cheek the day she chose Hilliard, knowing full well it could cost her everything. God told me He would resurrect my marriage. Not simply repair it. Not rebrand it for appearances. But resurrect it—from the grave, from the slow decay of disappointment, and from the depths of disbelief.

Just like He gave Emma a vision of a life beyond Letohatchee's fields, and just like He gave Hilliard the courage to choose her over inheritance and legacy—He gave me a promise no one could touch. He gave names, faces, and addresses. He gave me a vision of the other woman that broke

---

3. Psalm 121:3 NIV

up my marriage. She was riding in a car with a man whose name I didn't know, who hadn't even arrived at the same company they worked at yet—but two weeks later, he did.

And just as surely as Hilliard stood before the elders of Letohatchee and declared a love that could not be broken by the law, I stood before the silence of an empty house and declared a faith that could not be broken by betrayal.

Because God sings in strange keys—minor chords and unexpected cadences. And yet, His harmony never fails.

In 2014, after my mother transitioned and my marriage lay in ruins, God told me to *write.* To remember. To testify. To make public the private lyrics He had been humming over me since the day I was born.

Just as He preserved Emma and Hilliard's defiance in the marrow of descendants like me, He preserved mine in ink and page. He said, *"Publish it. Let the world see that I still keep My promises."* And so, I did, because when God marks something as a testimony, it cannot be silenced by disbelief.

Hilliard didn't just love Emma. He warred for her. And I don't just believe in God. I have had to war for what He said is mine.

God's love songs aren't always soft. Sometimes they are thunder. Sometimes they are courtroom confessions, front porch standoffs and burial clothes folded neatly for resurrection. But always—they are holy.

He said to me, *"I am parting the Red Sea for you, and the enemies you see today, you will see no more. Stand STILL… see how I deliver you and perform that which I have promised you."*

These were not just ancient words echoing from Sinai's past—they were the breath of God on my neck in the modern wilderness. I wasn't staring across desert sands or standing before Pharaoh's chariots, but I *was* standing at a sea—a vast divide between promise and impossibility.

The Spirit whispered again what Moses once shouted to a trembling people: *"Stand still and see the salvation of the Lord."* But when did he say this? Not when the path was clear, but when it looked like death itself. When the Hebrews were trapped between the army of their oppression and the unknown depth of the Red Sea—between the scars of their past and the still-unseen promise of their future.

That's where I stood. That's where *we* stand—every one of us who dares to believe in freedom while still smelling the smoke of bondage.

"My salvation," He said, *"always looks impossible. But what is impossible for man is possible with ME."*

And so I believed. I clung to it. I clung like Hilliard must have clung to Emma in the hush of night when whispers of freedom dared cross color lines, and when loving her was a crime punishable by shame or death. He defied the laws written by men because he had heard something greater whispered from Heaven. *Love is the law of My Kingdom*, God says, *and no man can undo what I ordain.*

God was parting something in me—then, and even now. *"I AM parting your Red Sea, and you will walk on dry land,"* He said. *"Then I will cause your enemies to be swallowed up by the Sea. Your Promised Land is on the other side. Walk through to the other side and receive your rest."*

Those words wrapped themselves around my bones in 2014, like prophecy etched in stone. At first, I thought they were only meant for me—for my restoration, for my husband, for my healing. But as the years passed and the tide of this nation began to shift, I realized God's song was never just about my solo. It was a symphony—for a people, for a generation, for a nation in need of remembering.

Then came January 20, 2025. It felt like a veil was torn the wrong way. The ink of reversal flowed with every stroke of the pen from a man who said we'd had enough—that nothing more was owed to the descendants of slaves, as if there had been some form of payment made. His statements rang as if the Liberty Bell had rung too many times for us and that the fight for freedom had already been won. But I knew better. I could feel it in the pit of my spirit.

What God had spoken to me wasn't just for my house—it was for the house of every son and daughter who has ever traced their lineage back to chains. The Red Sea He spoke of wasn't just the division between me and my husband—that was only *smoke and mirrors*. It was the chasm between justice and injustice, between freedom and whitewashed history, between America's delusion and God's deliverance.

Why did He give me a Hebraic promise? Because the bondage of Egypt and the brutality of the transatlantic slave trade are mirrors—distorted, bloodstained reflections of the same spirit of oppression. The difference? The Hebrews *left* Egypt. We never did.

We were freed in form, but not in foundation. Even now, the soul of this nation trembles at the idea of our liberation being complete. Even now, laws must be reauthorized every 25 years just to ensure we can *vote*. And even now, a President can erase progress with the stroke of a pen—and many of those cheering him on sing "Jesus loves me" without a trace of conviction.

But God said, "Stand still." Because He sees it all—the lynching of my uncle, the torment endured by my ancestors, and the betrayal etched into my own story. He sees the lashes. The nooses. He heard the lies told in Sunday school while Black bodies hung from trees like cursed fruit. And He is not silent. Not then. Not now. Not ever.

"Is there anything too hard for Me?" He asked me. No. Nothing. Not the healing of my heart. Not the resurrection of a dead marriage. Not even the reformation of a broken nation.

He said: *"The Winds of Change are blowing and everything is moving swiftly and with great momentum. Don't be moved by what you see and hear,"* says the Spirit of God.

So I stopped watching the news for confirmation. I stopped needing culture's approval or policy's permission. I tuned my ear to Heaven's frequency and heard Him say:

"Mark my words—dear daughter—I AM making a road in the wilderness. Your Way out has come—finally." And it was not just mine. It was Emma's. Hilliard's. It was Harriet's. It was Medgar's. It was Martin's. It was mine. It is ours.

"Suddenly! Suddenly everything is changing." We are shedding the weight of history's grief. No more wandering in the wilderness of white supremacy. No more missteps under systems designed for our failure. No more whispered apologies. No more survival as a substitute for freedom.

This is not revision. This is resurrection.

He said: *"This night, you will shed no more tears over this situation… As you raise your faith, I am causing your Red Sea to open up."* And so I walk— through parted waters that once seemed impassable. And I forgive. The slave master. The betrayer. The other woman. The system. The silence. Because in the Kingdom of Heaven, the forgiven *forgive*—and in doing so, we are made whole.

God made a promise to me. And as He weaves my pain with my ancestors' cry, I begin to understand that my story was never just mine. It is the story of *us*—of a people unbroken, a melody not silenced, and a love under new management.

I used to live by the creed, *"burn me once, shame on you; burn me twice, shame on me."* Now, I live by: *"love always hopes. Love always forgives. Love never fails."* Because real love isn't weak—it's a *weapon*. A shield. A testimony. And any weapon formed against us will not prosper.

Love shaped my story. Love redefined my enemies. Love taught me to walk through waters I once feared. And now I stand. Whole. Healed. Held. Not because the world changed. But because *I* did. Because *He* will do what He promised. Because God's love songs never fade.

Love is not always soft. Sometimes it bruises before it binds. Sometimes it breaks before it builds. Sometimes, it walks with bloody feet across ground not yet made holy.

In God's economy, love is a revolution. A remnant. A roar. It does not excuse injustice, but it transcends it. It is not blind to suffering—it stares it down and sings anyway.

From Emma and Hilliard's defiant love beneath the shadow of cotton fields, to my own journey through betrayal and restoration, God has revealed that love is more than emotion. It is endurance. It is more than romance. It is resistance. He is still writing love songs in the lives of those who dare to believe—songs that do not forget the past but refuse to be imprisoned by it.

The Red Sea is parting but the journey continues. And now we walk forward… with eyes wide open, and hands made clean by grace.

There are songs that soften the soul…And there are songs that shatter ceilings. But some songs—God's most haunting, most holy ones—are sung through *blood.* Not just the blood of Jesus, but the blood of those who bore His image and were crushed beneath the weight of injustice. The blood that cried out not just from Southern soil, but from all over this nation. From nooses. From knees. From courtrooms and cotton gins. The blood that was never truly washed away.

As we cross through the waters of the Red Sea, we step not into fantasy—but into *reckoning*. We cannot claim the Promised Land without confronting the price paid to reach it. We cannot shout "freedom" without mourning the ones who were silenced on the way.

And so, the next song is not a lullaby. It is a lament. It is *"Bloody Hands."* Let the truth be told.

My Prayer

Father, You are the Composer of every holy note, every divine refrain. You wrote the melody of my life before I ever knew how to sing. Thank You for the songs of deliverance You've placed around me, and the symphony of love You've stirred within me.

Thank You for walking me through waters meant to drown me, for restoring what was once buried, and for shaping me into a vessel You can trust to carry love into hard places. I confess: my hands have not always been clean. My heart has not always been soft. But You, O God, have purified both. Teach me to love like You love—Not selectively, but sacrificially. Not silently, but prophetically. Not weakly, but boldly. Give me grace for the next part of this journey. Let me not shrink back when I must speak truth. Let me not compromise when I must confront. Let me not forget that justice and love are twins in Your Kingdom.

In the name of Jesus—He who loved me when I was unlovable—Amen.

5

BLOODY HANDS

The blood cries out from the ground,
and it will not be silenced.

They say time heals all wounds. But what of wounds that were never dressed? What of bodies broken and buried without names, and generations forced to forget the smell of their own soil?

This is not a chapter about slavery as an idea. This is about slavery as a wound—still pulsing, still infected, and still splitting the skin of a country that insists it has healed.

The hands that picked cotton, bled into sugar, and built a nation's wealth were not just shackled—they were silenced. And those hands, long buried beneath polite history, are rising now, not to beg, but to testify.

These are bloody hands. The guilt rests not just on the hands of enslavers, but also on those who turned away. It lies with politicians who signed compromise after compromise. Churches that preached salvation but blessed the beatings and lynchings have bloody hands. Families who inherited land soaked in trauma and called it legacy have bloody hands.

You cannot wash away blood with time. You cannot clean it with silence. And you cannot build justice on soil that still screams.

This chapter is not a lullaby. It is a reckoning. They built monuments to the Confederacy before they ever built a memorial for the enslaved.

Stone and steel were raised in reverence to men who fought for the right to own people, while the people themselves were buried in unmarked graves behind barns, beneath roads, and beneath America. Nobody wanted to talk about the blood. They still don't.

It was easier to call it "the peculiar institution" than to name it what it was—terrorism, sanctioned and sanctified. It is easier to romanticize the plantations than to recount the screams that echoed between the rows of cotton. It is easier to speak of 'heritage' than to admit that the inheritance was stolen—harvested from the backs of men and women who were never paid for their services and were never meant to survive, only to serve.

They carved commemorations in honor of men who waged war for a lost cause long before they ever honored the men and women enslaved by it, as if defeat could be sanctified if wrapped in glory. They enshrined the defenders of bondage in marble and bronze, casting them as heroes while ignoring the broken bodies that bore the weight of a nation's wealth. The ones who toiled without mercy, and who built America brick by blood-stained brick, were left nameless—no statue, no stone, and not even a whispered remembrance in the soil they died on.

This is not history as they teach it. This is not the tidy version. This is the blood-soaked truth. Slavery was not a footnote—it was the foundation. They built a machinery of cruelty so refined, so calculated, that it turned flesh into currency and souls into ledger entries. Families were auctioned like cattle, whipped for learning, raped for breeding, and told it was the will of God.

And when the chains finally fell, they weren't replaced with freedom. They were replaced with laws, with vagrancy statutes, with lynch mobs, Jim Crow, and Black Codes. They were replaced with redlines, poll taxes, and the soft violence of "you're not welcome here."

Hands built this country—bloody hands. Hands, calloused from cotton and sugarcane, scarred by shackles, trembled with rage and memory.

And yet those same hands were blamed for the mess they were forced to clean.

They said, *"That was a long time ago."* As if time could erase a wound that was never allowed to close. As if injustice had an expiration date.

But blood doesn't lie. It seeps into the soil. It clings to deeds and documents, to bank vaults and family Bibles. It stains inheritances passed down through generations who never had to ask where the land came from or who paid the cost.

America perfected forgetting. They called it progress. But the fields remember. The trees remember. The rivers still carry the echoes of those who jumped rather than be broken. The church pews remember the sermons that blessed brutality. The courthouses remember the names never called for jury duty and for unfair judgments rendered against innocent people. The schools remember the lies. And every now and then, the memory rises like smoke.

You see it in the eyes of mothers burying their sons. It is steeped in textbooks scrubbed of rebellion. It is sustained by the denial of history by those still living on its dividends.

This isn't about guilt—it's about admission. It is the acknowledgment that no healing can happen without exposure, and that no true peace can come from pretending everything is fine.

The American dream was built on a nightmare. That is not a matter of opinion—it is a matter of arithmetic. Those who inherit privilege without reflection cannot claim innocence. Silence is not a neutral position. It is an alibi.

This chapter isn't for comfort. It's for confrontation. It's not asking for permission to speak—it's a demand that the truth be heard above the national anthem, the pledge of allegiance, and the sound of coins clinking in hands that have never known the weight of a whip.

This is not the end. This is the evidence. These are the bloody hands that built the republic. The Emancipation was signed with ink but lived with blood.

Freedom came with no land, no restitution, and no roadmap—just the ragged breath of people who had survived the unimaginable and were now told to start over with nothing. There were no reparations and no apologies. Only the same overseers now called sheriffs. The same fields now called sharecropping. The same plantations renamed "farms," still owned by the same families. And the freedmen—if they refused to work for wages too low to feed a child—were labeled lazy, while the men who had once owned them were honored as patriots.

They didn't hang the chains back on the bodies; they wrapped them around the systems. Through laws. Through courts. Through banks. The prisons filled as quickly as the slave ships once had. The Thirteenth Amendment abolished slavery, *except* as punishment for a crime—and suddenly, everything a freed Black man did was treated as a crime.

Standing on the corner was a crime. Reading was a crime. Looking a white woman in the eye was a crime. Voting was a crime.

The Reconstruction era promised justice, but it bled out fast—cut down by backlash, burned in church bombings, and shot through with assassinations. The Freedmen's Bureau was dismantled. Black lawmakers were driven from office. White mobs decided ballots didn't matter when they had bullets.

The schools built with sweat and sacrifice were torched. The Black Wall Streets were bombed. The newspapers that dared to print the truth were threatened or shut down. And through it all, the narrative remained the same: that Black people were the problem—that they asked for too much and rose too fast.

And when resistance came—as it *always* did—it was labeled as savagery. It was framed as riot rather than revolt, as criminality instead of self-defense. From Harper's Ferry to Tulsa, from Watts to Ferguson, the script never changed. The story was always rewritten to vilify the oppressed and vindicate the oppressor.

Meanwhile, white America perfected the art of erasure. They told stories of happy slaves, benevolent masters, and loyal mammies who rocked white babies while their own children went hungry. They turned plantations into wedding venues. They called slave quarters "guest houses." They turned trauma into tourism.

But the truth does not die. It waits—patiently. It remains in the soil, in the bloodline, and in the eyes of descendants who carry both the burden and the brilliance of those who were never meant to survive—and yet did.

The war never ended. It just changed uniforms. Today, the battleground looks different, but the fight is the same. It lives in redlined neighborhoods and under-funded schools. It hides in police budgets that grow larger than libraries, and in voting districts carved like cages. It moves in the currency of suspicion, in the subtle nods of exclusion, and in the systemic denial of full humanity. But freedom has never been a gift. It has always been a battle.

And still, they rise—those whose ancestors were once bartered and branded. They rise with memory in their marrow, and resistance in their breath. They rise knowing that survival was never the goal. What they sought—what they still seek—is something greater: dignity, ownership, rest, joy, and the power to reclaim what was taken.

Let no one say the past is past. The past is alive. It is active. It is armed and legislated and the only thing more dangerous than forgetting... is pretending it never happened.

The hands are still bloody, but they are no longer bound. They changed the tools, not the target. Today, it's not whips but wage gaps. Not auction blocks, but housing deeds stamped with red lines invisible to the eye but sharp enough to cut down generations. The cotton fields are now classrooms where Black children are over-policed and under-funded. The patrols on horseback now wear badges. They still chase. They still shoot. And the system still protects them.

A Black man is still not allowed to run without suspicion. A Black woman is still not allowed to rest without dying in her sleep. Being unarmed means nothing. Complying means nothing. Even hands raised in surrender mean nothing— when the very sight of your body is treated as a threat.

America is still at war, with its own shadow. It chants equality while it legislates exclusion. It waves the flag while gutting voting rights. It preaches peace but funds brutality. And then, when the wounded cry out, it tells them to do it quieter, to be more polite, to kneel in a way that doesn't offend the very boot pressing down on their neck.

This country has always demanded the oppressed bleed with dignity. Even protest is policed—not just by the state, but by the collective conscience of a nation that would rather sleep than reckon. They say slavery ended, as if chains can't morph into policies. As if the plantation didn't just evolve into a prison complex, a loan rejection, a denied job application, and a death by neglect in a city hospital.

But here is the truth they cannot bury: the blood never dried. It is in the streets named after men who wrote laws to keep Black families broken. It is in textbooks that skip from 1865 to Martin Luther King Jr. as if a hundred years of terror, resistance, and systemic oppression never happened in between. It exists in corporate offices where boardrooms remain all white. It shows up in hospitals, where Black women die during childbirth at three times the rate of white women. It echoes in courtrooms where justice is handed out like punishment, not protection.

And yet, Black life persists—not because the system allows it, but in spite of it. In spite of centuries of being told they were less—less capable, less worthy, less human—Black people have dared to dream, to write, to build, to lead, and to love radically. They have taught their children who they are before the world tells them who they are not.

They write poetry in protest. They build futures in fire-scorched soil. They laugh, loudly and unapologetically, in the face of a country that only seems to value Black culture when it can be sold, and Black pain when it can be dismissed.

This is not resilience as performance. This is survival as resistance. This is the gospel of a people who understand that hope is not gentle. It bears scars, carries weight, and is forged through struggle—not ease.

So when America says, *"Let's move on,"* this chapter answers, *"To what?"* You cannot move forward without looking back. You cannot build justice on bones you refuse to acknowledge. And you cannot wash your hands clean when the foundation of your house is soaked in someone else's blood.

The hands are still bloody, and they have never stopped being. They were bloody when they signed the emancipation and left Black families with no land, and no restitution—only hunger and the illusion of freedom. They were bloody when they lit the torches in Rosewood, in Wilmington, and in Tulsa—when entire Black towns were razed to the ground and called "race riots" to protect the killers. They were bloody when they wrapped nooses around Black necks and called it justice. And they are still bloody now.

They were bloody when they shot Tamir for holding a toy. Bloody when they broke into Breonna's home and filled it with bullets, then silence. Bloody when they choked the life out of George Floyd on camera, for the world to see, and still asked for context. Bloody when Ahmaud was hunted through the streets, lynched in broad daylight—not with a burning cross, but with a cell phone recording every moment.

There was no white hood. No burning tree. Just a badge. Just a pickup truck. Just a law, written to protect the hands that killed.

America never stopped lynching Black bodies—it simply changed the method, the headlines, and the excuse. Now the justification sounds like this: "He was resisting," "She had a record," or "They feared for their life." The noose was replaced with a narrative, but the outcome remains the same. Fear is not neutral. It is taught. And taught fear always finds its way back to the trigger.

Meanwhile, Black grief is expected to be graceful. Families are told to forgive before they can even bury their dead. Entire communities are told to protest peacefully while bleeding. And when the protest rises anyway—raw, fiery, unstoppable—the nation clutches its pearls, not because of the injustice, but because the mirror finally cracked.

Bloody hands are not just the ones that kill—they're the ones that defend the killers. The ones that write policies to protect power. The ones that turn off body cams. The ones that edit footage. The ones that place knees on necks and call it protocol.

This is not the past repeating. It's the past *never ending*. From the trees to the asphalt, from the lynching rope to the police baton, the Black body has never been allowed to simply *be*—to walk, to drive, to sleep, or just to breathe.

And still, they ask why the hands are raised. Why the fists are clenched. Why the wounds won't close. The answer is carved into the soil, etched into the walls of courtrooms, and buried in the silence that follows every press conference that ends with *"no charges filed."*

This nation's hands are soaked in the blood of people it claims to be equal. And until that blood is reckoned with—not just acknowledged but accounted for—it will keep crying out from the ground like Abel's did in Genesis. And God is asking again, *"Where is your brother?"*

The blood still cries, and the hands remain bloody—not only in textbooks or black-and-white photographs, but in our own bloodlines. The stories are passed down at kitchen tables, whispered quietly and often left unfinished, because speaking them too clearly might still invite death.

This is one of those stories. My mother's father—my grandfather—worked in Birmingham, Alabama. Steel country. A place where men broke their backs for a dollar, if they were lucky, and for fifty cents if they were

Black. He and his son—my uncle—worked for the same company. Hard men. Honest men. Men who knew how to keep their heads down and their mouths shut, until silence was no longer possible.

Some of the white men at that company made more money than others—not because they worked harder, but because they were white and they ran moonshine across state lines. It was illegal, yes, but profitable and white privilege cloaked it in protection.

When my uncle found out, he didn't ask for much—only what he felt was fair. If they were getting paid extra for illegal labor, he asked to be included. He wasn't trying to cause trouble; he was trying to feed his family. He believed, perhaps naively, that fairness might still find a place in a dirty deal.

But the bloody hands don't like to be challenged. They don't like when Black men speak with backbone. So, they gave him a shift—early morning before the sun rose. They told him to come in before the others. They told him there was extra work for him.

That was their opportunity. They lynched him before the morning whistle blew—not in a distant field or under a burning cross but quietly, cleanly. It was the kind of Southern violence that leaves no fingerprints, only silence.

My grandfather showed up for work that same morning, likely with lunch in a paper bag. He was likely humming a hymn under his breath. He came expecting a day like any other—and instead, walked into a nightmare that would never end.

His son was dead, and he knew who did it. Everyone did. There were no strangers on that shift, no anonymous shadows. The very men who took his son's life would swing hammers beside him for years to come. They would laugh, eat, and collect their paychecks signed in blood.

And he kept working there. It was not out of fear but because there was no safety net. There was no therapist to help him process the trauma, and there was certainly no court or justice to make things right. There was only a man, trying to hold together what little he had left, while walking through the wreckage of everything that had been stolen from him.

Imagine the weight he carried—the grief, the rage, and the restraint it took to show up every day and not set the building on fire. The idea that he had to hear the killers breathe, cough, clear their throats, and go on living is unimaginable.

They didn't just kill his son. They forced him to carry the murder in silence. He was bound by them to sit with it. He was compelled by duty to shake hands with it. It was mandatory that he clock in beside it and cash checks soaked with it.

This is what America does to Black families. It breaks them, then demands their silence. It buries their children, then expects them to show up the next day as if nothing happened. It devastates, then dares them to keep moving—quiet, compliant, and unseen.

They call it resilience. But it is not. It is survival under siege. It is dignity under a boot. It is faith forged in fire so deep it burns generations. And still, they ask why we say the hands are bloody. We say it because it's true. Because they have always been. Because the bleeding doesn't stop when the headlines fade, when the papers are filed, or when the company quietly shuts its doors.

The blood follows us. It lives in our marrow. It cries out through generations who carry more than names; they carry wounds. So no—we do not forget. We remember, with bated breath, and we name the blood.

There is a grief so deep that it never finds language. There is a pain so generational it becomes part of the bone.

My grandfather's silence was not weakness—it was resistance. It was a refusal to lose his mind on top of his son. It was a man standing in the ruins of justice, still choosing to work, and still choosing to live.

But what do we do with blood that won't wash off? We carry it. We confront it. We testify with it. Because the bloody hands of this nation will never be cleansed by denial—not when they are stained with the breath of the lynched, the burned, and the broken.

History is not healed by forgetting. It is healed by truth. And that truth is ours to carry now—not as a burden, but as a banner. We are called to name the names, to speak what was never meant to be spoken, and to make the world remember what it worked so hard to erase.

We are the living proof that blood did not silence us. We are still standing. And we are still speaking. They tried to kill us. They failed. This blood did not stop with the grave—it rose through song, through movement, and through the unbreakable will of a people who refused to die quietly.

The next chapter is not just about pain. It is about power. It is about the melody that rose in the dark. The sound of a mother's voice echoed in the wilderness, teaching her children how to survive with nothing but a song.

And so, we move from blood to breath. We move from silence to sound, from the tree to the tambourine. We move from *A Mother's Melody* to *Bloody Hands*.

They told us to pull ourselves up by our bootstraps. But how do you pull yourself up when all you've ever been handed are *bloody hands*? Hands torn by chains, worn thin in cotton fields, and trembling under the weight of grief. They were the hands that buried sons. They were the hands that built cities. They were the hands that fed the nation and were left empty.

The lie of the bootstrap was never about empowerment; it was about erasure. It pretended there had been a fair start, a level field, and a clean slate. But there was no slate. There were only shackles, only graves, and only laws that declared, *"You're free,"* while crossing their fingers behind their backs.

They gave us nothing. They gave no land, no inheritance, and no protection. And then they had the audacity to blame us for falling behind.

This is not laziness. This is sabotage. And the next chapter tells the truth about that sabotage—about what happens when a people rise with *bloody hands*, only to be told their boots are broken, and that it's their fault they can't climb.

So, we move now—from the tree to the factory floor, from the field to the welfare line, from lynch mobs to loan denials, and from *Bloody Hands* to *Busted Bootstraps*.

6

BUSTED
BOOTSTRAPS

*"But let justice roll down like waters, and
righteousness like a mighty stream."*

Amos 5:24, kjv

They love to say it, don't they? "Pull yourself up by your bootstraps."
They speak it as if poverty is a personal failure, as if survival under
oppression is simply a lack of effort, and as if equity can be achieved through
sheer willpower in a system built to exploit. But the phrase itself—*"pull
yourself up by your bootstraps"*—was never meant to be motivational. It was
originally intended as a joke, a sarcastic reference to a literal impossibility:
someone trying to lift themselves off the ground by tugging on the very
straps attached to their own feet.

That's the foundation of the American Dream—an illusion built on
contradiction. A bootless people were told to climb. An uneducated people
bound and beaten were told to run the same race. And when they couldn't
keep up, they were blamed for their position on the track.

Let's be clear: white wealth in this country was not built by hard work
alone. It was built through land grants and stolen labor, through the
Homestead Act and redlining. It came from GI Bills that elevated white

veterans while excluding Black ones. It came from banks that financed white futures and denied Black dreams. They were not pulling themselves up by their bootstraps—they were being lifted by the hands of Uncle Sam.

Meanwhile, Black people were emancipated without reparations. They were set free without land, without tools, and without boots—then expected to compete in a game where the rules were written in invisible ink, legible only to those already winning. The hypocrisy is staggering. The arrogance is even thicker.

They pretend their ancestors tamed wildernesses—forgetting that enslaved hands cleared the land, built the homes, planted the fields, and raised their children. They tell us to work harder while standing on scaffolds built from our suffering.

So no, this is not about laziness. This is not about grit. This is about the lie at the center of the American myth—that everyone had a fair shot.

They didn't. We didn't. And until we tear down that lie, root and all, we will keep asking the wrong questions of the wrong people. The system was never broken. It was designed this way. And now, it must be confronted.

They said we didn't try hard enough. They claimed we wanted something for nothing, that we waited for handouts instead of putting in the work. But here's the truth they refuse to print in their history books: *we worked*. We worked until our backs split open and our children starved beside us. We worked while others inherited land, capital, and generational wealth, while we inherited debt, trauma, and silence.

We didn't fail to pull ourselves up by our bootstraps—*we were never given boots* to begin with. After Emancipation, they called us free, but freedom without land, restitution, shelter, wages, or protection was nothing more than abandonment dressed in patriotism.

The same government that gave away millions of acres to white settlers gave Black people nothing but sermons about thrift and patience.

While white veterans returned from war to FHA loans and GI Bill–funded homes, Black veterans returned to segregated streets, denied mortgages, and locked out of prosperity.

And when we built anyway—when we founded businesses, established schools, and raised churches—they bombed them, burned them, and blamed us for rising too fast. They said our ambition was a threat. So we worked the jobs no one else wanted. We picked the fields, laid the bricks, and paved the roads. Still, they called us lazy.

They underpaid us, then punished us for being poor. They exploited our labor, then criminalized our need. They broke our backs and then dared us to stand taller. And when we demanded equality, they handed us shame.

They taught our children to believe their struggle was personal, not political. They insisted that poverty was proof of laziness, not the product of a rigged system. But you don't get to break a people's legs and then blame them for limping.

This chapter is not about excuses—it is about evidence. It is about how the bootstraps were busted from the beginning and how the system was never built for us to rise. And yet, rise we did.

Freedom came without tools—no land, no education, no wages, no restitution. We received no compensation for centuries of stolen labor—just a pat on the back and a boot pressed to our necks.

In 1865, when the chains fell, America stood at a crossroads: to repair the harm or to repeat it. The Thirteenth Amendment declared us free. The Fourteenth promised citizenship. We clung to those words and fought to make them real. But the promise of Reconstruction collapsed beneath the weight of white rage. Lynch mobs hunted our bodies. Terrorists torched our towns. Even white allies were driven into silence.

The federal government, eager to reconcile with Confederate traitors who had drenched the nation in blood, turned its back on us. They handed power back to the same men who had enslaved us, and in their hands, freedom became a mockery. Racial terror became the rule, and Jim Crow the law of the land.

This nation chose repetition—wrapped in red, white, and blue. They promised us forty acres and a mule. A sliver of land. A chance. A beginning. But even that was stolen.

Confederate land—briefly given to the newly freed—was quickly reclaimed and returned to those who had waged war to preserve slavery. And the government told us, "Figure it out." We did. But every time we figured it out, they tore it down.

Generational wealth begins with ownership: of land, homes, and businesses. But for Black Americans, ownership has always been an uphill war. Banks denied us loans. Titles were forged. Deeds were challenged. Entire communities—like Blackdom, Oklahoma, and Rosewood, Florida—were burned off the map when Black families became "too successful."

Meanwhile, white families were accumulating wealth through policy. The *Homestead Act of 1862*[4] gave over *270 million acres of stolen Indigenous land to white settlers for free*. That land became capital, homes, farms, and generational inheritance.

Black families received nothing—no land, no equity, no access, no pathway to the American dream. And when we built anyway, they called us thieves. When we pooled our resources, they called it suspicious. When we demanded access, they said, "Wait your turn." But our turn never came.

The *GI Bill* is often hailed as a ladder to the middle class, but for Black veterans, that ladder was rigged. State and local officials routinely denied them access to the educational and housing benefits they had earned. Meanwhile, the *FHA* insured millions of home loans—so long as the buyers were white and the neighborhoods remained segregated. Red lines were

---

4. Congress. (n.d.). *Homestead act (1862)*. National Archives and Records Administration. https://www.archives.gov/milestone-documents/homestead-act

drawn across maps like scars, dividing communities by invisible boundaries with devastating consequences.

This was not a glitch in the system. It was the blueprint. The wealth gap we see today was not born from laziness—it was legislated. It was encoded in housing policies, banking regulations, and labor laws. It was upheld in courtrooms and protected by silence.

Today, the average white family holds ten times the wealth of the average Black family. It wasn't because one worked harder, but because one had a 400-year head start—and a nation holding the ladder.

So, no—do not talk to us about bootstraps; not while you walk on roads we paved, live on land we were never allowed to own, and profit from systems designed to keep us below. There was no inheritance for us— only loss. Only theft. Only deeds that led to denial and dreams stripped bare. But even without titles, land, or trust funds, Black families passed down something more powerful: memory, resistance, and fire. And the fire never died.

Slavery didn't end. It evolved. They swapped the whip for a ledger, the auction block for a work contract, and the plantation for the mill. They called it freedom—but it looked like the same chains, polished and renamed.

Sharecropping was slavery with a contract. They said, "Work the land and keep a share." But the land wasn't ours. Neither were the tools, the seed, the mule, or the market. Everything was owned and controlled by the same people who once owned our bodies. At the end of every season, we owed more than we began with. Every single year.

That wasn't misfortune. That was a strategy. The landowners kept the books, cooked the numbers, and inflated the prices. And if you challenged it, you vanished. You would be jailed, beaten, or left hanging from a tree— a warning dressed in flesh.

Then came the factories and the foundries—especially in places like Birmingham, Pittsburgh, and Detroit. Black men were given the most dangerous jobs with the lowest wages and no protections. They were worked to the bone with no unions, no pensions, and no questions asked. When their bodies broke, the companies tossed them aside like tools dulled by use.

White workers had routes to retirement, promotion, and paid vacations. Black workers had broom closets and pink slips. And when they organized, when they dared to speak, they were called ungrateful, unruly, or worse—a threat. Some died from the labor. Some died from the waiting.

Women were not spared. They labored as maids, laundresses, cooks, and caretakers—raising white children while their own went hungry. They scrubbed floors in homes they could never afford, served families who would never serve them, and when their bodies broke from too many years bent over in silence, no one noticed. No one came.

There was always one unspoken rule: Black women could be used, but never truly seen. Even when we built our own businesses—barbershops, rail lines, print shops, farms, grocery stores—our success was met with sabotage. These ventures were bombed, boycotted, or bought out for scraps. Our independence was perceived as a threat to white dominance.

The cycle was brutal and unrelenting: work, starve, work more, borrow, be denied, work harder, and die poor. And then they had the audacity to ask, "Why can't you get ahead?" Because the game was never fair and it was never meant to be.

This is what economic bondage looks like in a country that swears it's free: A man working three jobs and still losing his home. A woman caring for someone else's children while her own raise themselves. A generation told to dream, then priced out of the promise before it even began.

And still—we worked. We worked for dignity. We worked because there was no other option. We worked knowing the deck was stacked, but we played our hand anyway. Because hope is not the absence of struggle; it is the refusal to surrender.

They called us moochers, beggars, and welfare queens. They broke our backs, then mocked us for needing a crutch.

The same system that stole our wealth turned around and blamed us for having none. The same government that denied us land, loans, and living wages offered crumbs—and crucified us for accepting them.

Welfare was never a handout. It was a setup. It came wrapped in strings, steeped in shame, and saturated with surveillance.

The earliest welfare programs were created to serve white widows, white orphans, and white farmers. But when Black mothers—pushed there by segregation, starvation, and exclusion—entered the system, it suddenly became a "problem" that needed fixing.

They policed our motherhood. They inspected our homes. They placed limits on how many children we could have, on what kind of man—if any—was allowed in the house, and on what kind of work we could pursue.

They sent social workers to count toothbrushes and bedsheets. They monitored for signs of "male presence." They turned food into evidence. They turned survival into suspicion. And from that suspicion, they created the myth.

The myth of the "*Welfare Queen*" was a calculated lie—stitched from white fear and upheld by white supremacy. A caricature of a Black woman, lazy and greedy, was created not to reflect truth but to serve political agendas, media ratings, and public scapegoating. Entire campaigns were launched in her name. Entire safety nets were dismantled because of her image. But she was never the failure. The failure was the system that made her necessary.

White Americans, in fact, *benefit most from welfare programs*. The greatest welfare system this country has ever seen is not food stamps—but *tax breaks for the wealthy*. Yet the face of public aid was painted Black, intentionally, so that the fight for economic justice could be vilified and racialized. As long as white working-class citizens were convinced that Black people were the problem, no one would look up and question the real thieves of prosperity.

This was never about fiscal responsibility—it was about control, punishment and shame. They wanted our gratitude for scraps, our silence in suffering, our invisibility in pain. But we turned food stamps into lifelines. Section 8 homes became sanctuaries. What they meant to humiliate us only proved our ability to survive. Survival itself became resistance.

If freedom was the promise, wealth was supposed to be the proof. But every time we reached for it, the rules changed. The lines moved. The gate grew taller. In America, wealth is not just money. It is ownership, leverage, and security—the power to pass something down. But for Black families, the starting line was deliberately set out of reach. And when we got close, they burned it down.

Redlining was quiet theft. Maps drawn in red ink coded Black neighborhoods as "hazardous," and banks followed those maps religiously. A Black family with perfect credit could still be denied a loan simply because of their zip code. Home ownership—our clearest path to generational wealth—was blocked by policy, not merit. And when we managed to buy homes anyway, values dropped, services disappeared, and new traps emerged.

Owner-financed homes became the last resort—packaged as opportunity but rigged with predatory terms. White families became the banks. "Creative financing" was simply a new form of exploitation, designed to extract wealth without offering equity. And still, we dared to dream. We endured scrutiny, bias, and humiliation—not out of trust, but necessity.

It was never a glitch. It was architecture.

Predatory lending, subprime mortgages, and balloon payments followed. Even those who qualified for better were steered into worse. Foreclosures swept through Black neighborhoods like a plague—not because we failed, but because the system was built for us to fail.

In the *workforce*, Black resumes were tossed for sounding "too ethnic." Promotions rarely came. Pay rarely matched labor. Entrepreneurs faced barriers at every turn—fewer loans, less protection, and more suspicion. A white man could fail and get funded again. A successful Black woman was met with audits and accusations.

Then came *mass incarceration*—modern slavery in a posturing, post-racial world. Communities were drained of fathers, workers, and leaders. Men were locked away for nonviolent offenses and stripped of their rights long after release. Incarceration didn't just take bodies—it stole wealth, dismantled families, and severed generations. It was theft, dressed up as justice.

So when they ask why the wealth gap exists, the answer is not elusive. It's intentional. They drew the maps. They wrote the laws. They issued the loans. They owned the banks, the deeds, the courts, the schools, and the narrative.

This was never accidental. It was by design. And now—we name it. We refuse to carry their shame. We carry truth. We carry fire.

This was never about failure—it was about fencing the future. It was about locking Black families out while white wealth stacked itself higher, generation after generation. Yet even when the gates were closed, the ladders pulled up, and the loans denied, we kept building. We built not just homes, but hope, not just businesses, but belief, not just survival, but a blueprint for something better.

They hoarded the land, the labor, and the wealth. Then they handed us the blame. Shame became the final chain—no longer around our wrists, but around our minds. They called us broken, and we began to wonder if it was true. They called us lazy, and we worked ourselves to exhaustion trying to prove otherwise. They whispered that we were less, and we carried that lie in our blood, our breath, and our backs.

We measured ourselves by rulers never meant for us. We asked each other why we hadn't "made it out," instead of asking who designed the trap. This is the violence that goes deeper than laws—this is psychological warfare. It convinces the oppressed that they are the problem. It breaks the spirit even when the body survives.

Our parents told us to be twice as good—not because the system was fair, but because they knew excellence might be the only armor we had. So we dressed our trauma in degrees, in diction, and in discipline. We masked pain with professionalism and swallowed rage behind polite smiles. But no code-switch, no résumé, no Ivy League degree ever stopped a bullet or silenced a badge.

When we fall—and we will, because the foundation was never made to hold us—they call it proof. They quote statistics with no story. They cite dropout rates without naming disinvestment. They blame crime without indicting poverty, policing, and policy. They treat poverty like a personality flaw and trauma like a family tradition. They twist our survival into dysfunction and ask us to be grateful for the struggle.

Let the record be set straight: the shame was never ours. It belongs to the men who passed down wealth built on whips and wars. It belongs to the lawmakers who fed injustice breath by breath. We were not broken—we were betrayed. Still, we rise. We're not bearing shame, but sacred memory. We are not carrying guilt, but grit. Still, we hope—because our ancestors did not survive the impossible so we could live small.

This is not our shame. This is our story. And we will not apologize for surviving it.

They thought they buried us. But Blackness does not die. It multiplies. It sings. It rises. It remembers. What they called failure was resistance all along.

When they stole the land, we made gardens out of dust. When they barred us from their banks, we built our own. When they locked us out of their schools, we taught in basements and on porches. When they turned our neighborhoods into war zones, we turned street corners into sanctuaries.

We resisted through lullabies and laments. Through hand-me-down books and secondhand dreams. Through worship and work. Through laughter and longing. And we resisted simply by breathing—by refusing to disappear. Because the most dangerous thing a broken system can face is a people who know they were never broken.

They tried to shame the Black woman, yet she became our backbone. They tried to cage the Black man, yet he emerged as a mirror, a prophet, and a storm. They sought to suppress and oppress both, but Black women and men became the pillars of American society. They tried to silence the Black child, and that child rose as a scholar, a singer, a spark of resistance.

We descend from those who were never meant to read, yet they wrote poetry. We come from those who were never meant to speak, yet they shaped the soul of culture. We are the offspring of those who were never meant to vote, yet they changed the course of history. While they passed down trust funds, we passed down fire.

That fire burned in choir stands and courtroom pews. It stirred in the movements, the marches, and the music. It lives in the whispered wisdom of grandmothers, and in the thunder of freeborn children still fighting for the promise their birth should have secured.

Yes, we inherited trauma—but we also inherited triumph. We inherited ingenuity, forged not in luxury but in wilderness. Our faith was not handed to us—it was carved from silence and sanctified by survival. This is our legacy: not bootstraps, but blueprints—not a tale of rags to riches, but ashes to resurrection.

We did not merely pull ourselves up—we built our own ladders while being pushed from the rooftop. Even now, we are still building. From busted bootstraps and broken promises, we have stitched together lives of meaning. We have borne burdens we did not create, walked through fires we did not ignite, and survived systems designed to erase us. But survival is not the end of the story. It never was.

There comes a time when endurance is no longer enough—when silence becomes betrayal, when patience becomes permission, when stillness becomes surrender. That time is now. We've been told to wait, to pray, to behave, to be grateful for scraps. But we were never created to crawl.

There is something rising in our bones—older than protest, deeper than policy. This is not rage for the sake of rage. This is not vengeance dressed as virtue. This is sacred. This is a holy rebellion.

A rebellion against the lies we were fed. Against the shame we were taught. Against systems that wear civility like a disguise and injustice like a badge.

This next chapter is not about vengeance—it is about vision. It is about reclaiming what was never theirs to own: our voice, our dignity, and our destiny. From fields to factories, from ghettos to grandmothers' porches, from blood-stained streets to sanctified pulpits—we are rising—not in riot, but in righteousness, not with bootstraps, but with boldness, not in fear, but in fire.

Welcome to the uprising. Welcome to the next chapter. Welcome to *A Holy Rebellion*.

This is not a rebellion of chaos—but of clarity, not one born of destruction—but of resurrection. This rebellion begins in the spirit, where righteousness stands firm and refuses to bow to corruption. And every rebellion needs a battleground.

Ours is covered in cracked concrete and empty lots. It is steeped in boarded windows and shattered glass. It lingers in liquor stores on every corner, and in hope hidden behind padlocked doors. The war was never just waged with bullets—it was fought with bulldozers, not with tanks, but with city council votes.

They didn't just break our families—they dismantled our neighborhoods. Then they renamed the wreckage "blight." They allowed our blocks to wither, then blamed us for the decay. They stole the tax base, closed the clinics, disinvested in schools, and criminalized our survival.

Let's make this plain—blight is not nature. It is policy. It is profit. It is punishment.

Now, the very system that abandoned these streets returns with developers dressed as saviors—not to restore us, but to sell us out.

But here is what they never expected: that the rebellion would take root right here. In these people. In these ashes.

They saw decay. We see sacred ground. They saw loss. We see legacy. Because beneath the ruin, the soil still remembers. The children still dream. The elders still pray.

This is not just about urban neglect—it is about spiritual betrayal. About how a nation turned its back on its prophets, its poor, and its people—and how we are reclaiming what was left for dead.

They called it blight. But we call it holy ground. *Welcome to The Plight of Blight.* The age of discovery was more like the age of exploitation.

7

PLIGHT OF BLIGHT

We are not the ruins of the past; we are the
architects of what must come next.

They didn't simply abandon our neighborhoods; they executed them. Under the false banners of "urban renewal" and "economic development," they arrived with clipboards and bulldozers, armed with blueprints that erased us. They tore down our homes, carved up our streets, and buried our history beneath concrete and broken promises. Then they stepped back, called it progress, and watched the rot they planted take root.

This was never accidental decay. It was deliberate destruction. They poisoned the soil, then blamed the ones left struggling to grow anything in the dust. And sometimes the violence came not with wrecking balls, but with paperwork and deception. I know this truth not just from history books, but from the quiet testimony passed down in my family.

It was 1969 when my parents made the brave decision to move across town—from Atlanta to Decatur, Georgia—in search of something better. A new beginning. A place where their children could thrive beyond what they had ever known. That Christmas, before we moved, one of our neighbors stole every single Christmas gift from our home. Then, as if to make a spectacle of their theft, they rode our bikes and skated with our skates in their front yard, daring us to challenge what they already believed: that we had no right to expect better.

My father was furious—but he was not broken. He resolved to find a neighborhood with better schools, broader opportunity, and a future that could not be stolen from beneath our feet.

He was a veteran of World War II. He had excellent credit. He was responsible and prepared. But none of that mattered.

The banks refused him—not because of numbers, but because of color. The doors that opened wide for white borrowers slammed shut in his face. Still, he pressed on.

Eventually, he found a white homeowner willing to sell—someone eager to leave now that the neighborhood's racial line had been crossed. The only option was owner-financing, which came at a steep cost: a higher interest rate, an unspoken penalty for Black aspiration. Still, the terms were manageable. It was a sacrifice he was willing to make.

What we didn't know then—but would learn soon after—was that we were only the third Black family on that street. The ink was barely dry on our deed before "For Sale" signs began to sprout like weeds. White flight swept through the block like a storm. The old world refused to share space. Instead, it fled.

My parents paid eighteen thousand dollars for that house. It sat on over an acre of land, with four bedrooms, two bathrooms, a basement, a screened-in porch, a full-length patio, and a garage. To them, it was a palace. And it was theirs—not because anyone handed it to them, but because they refused to be denied.

We lived there for sixteen years. We celebrated milestones, made memories, and endured hardship. We invested in it—renovations, repairs, upgrades—all with their own hands, because no one else would.

After my father died and we had all grown, my mother chose to move on. She sold the house for a little over one hundred thousand dollars—a profit that, at the time, felt like a victory. But victory is often a matter of perspective.

The new owners flipped the house just two years later for two hundred thousand. Today, that same house is valued at 1.4 million dollars.

How does a house double in price in two years? How does it increase more than tenfold in a generation?

This is not the invisible hand of the market. It is exploitation dressed up as math, theft wearing the mask of capitalism, and exploitation disguised as economic growth. This is how Black wealth is stolen—quietly, legally, and repeatedly.

They call it gentrification now, as if dressing theft in modern language makes it moral. But it's the same old robbery—an ancient injustice wearing a polished face.

They saw what we had built—what we had nurtured through sweat, sacrifice, and silent strength—and they came back for it. They saw the size of the lots, the excellence of the schools, and the beauty we had preserved when they turned away. And they decided they wanted it again. This time, though, they came not with torches and mobs, but with real estate agents, appraisers, and glossy brochures.

My mother wasn't thinking about property appreciation or generational wealth. She just wanted peace and simplicity. The buyers saw dollar signs. And just like that, as had happened to countless others, we were pushed out of the very harvest we had planted.

Our neighborhood was never blighted—not in spirit or in soul. But many of my childhood friends grew up in places labeled as such. And when developers showed up, flashing cash to tired homeowners, it felt like a blessing. Many took the first offer without knowing the value of their property, unaware that they could have asked for double—or triple—and still had willing buyers. No one had ever told them they could demand more—and receive it.

What they called blight was not just decaying buildings or crumbling sidewalks. It was the systemic devaluation of Black space, Black labor, and Black dreams. They taught us to believe that our communities held no worth and then came to buy them cheap. But the earth remembers. The ruins still speak. The seeds we planted—buried in stolen soil—continue to live.

Our story is not isolated. It is a single stitch in a much larger fabric of forced displacement. Across this nation, in city after city, it happened the same way. They called it "urban renewal," but those it uprooted knew the truth: it was "Negro removal."

Highways cut through the hearts of Black communities—not for traffic relief, but for economic expansion. Entire neighborhoods were labeled slums—not because of their condition, but because of the people who lived in them. With one denial here, one foreclosure there, a widened street, a rerouted highway, and a razed block, Black communities were dismantled—piece by piece.

They drained resources, denied credit, and let infrastructure crumble. Then, when the effects of their neglect became undeniable, they labeled it "blight" and declared it ripe for redevelopment. And when we tried to rebuild—when the children of the displaced returned with hope in hand—we found the doors still locked, the pens still poisoned, and the theft still silent.

Now the hollowed houses and cracked church steeples stand as testimony. Every boarded window, every weed-choked yard, every empty storefront tells the truth they tried to bury: this was never about helping us. The blight was not organic. It was orchestrated. And the land has not forgotten.

Street by street, our communities were gutted under the banner of "progress." Demolition crews leveled homes where generations had lived and loved. What followed wasn't a rebirth, but a wasteland—a graveyard of dreams, littered with broken promises and broken glass.

They called it blight. As if the bricks decayed themselves. As if the boards nailed themselves across windows. As if our communities woke up one morning and chose ruin. But we know the truth. And so does the land.

Blight is not a condition. It is a code. A word wrapped in policy and soaked in fear. It translates to: "Too Black," "Not profitable," and "Let it rot." And they made it so.

When the factories closed and the jobs disappeared, when the tax base eroded and the landlords vanished while still collecting rent, the city didn't call it abandonment. They called it "urban decline"—as if decline were a storm and not a strategy.

They spoke of our neighborhoods like they were corpses: "blighted," "decaying," "high-crime zones." But the crime came after the starvation. The decay followed the divestment. And the blight? That was the story they crafted to excuse their betrayal. Once they declared a neighborhood "blight," they no longer had to fix it. Once they labeled the place, they stopped loving it.

When we organized, painted murals, planted gardens, and fought to preserve what we had, they told us to be grateful that anyone still wanted to invest. As if our resilience wasn't already sacred. As if our children weren't miracles growing in salted soil.

This wasn't decay. It was neglect draped in real estate jargon. It was theft hiding behind clipboards and paperwork. It was violence without a weapon—but with just as many funerals.

Redlining came first. Banks and government offices drew maps in red, marking Black neighborhoods as "high risk"—not because of crime, but because of race. There were no loans, no insurance, and no investment. Instead, there was a message written in ink and enforced by law: *"Don't build here, don't grow here, and don't care here."*

Then came disinvestment. The jobs dried up. The taxes vanished. The infrastructure cracked. Streetlights dimmed. Sidewalks buckled. Trash overflowed, and nobody came. Schools were gutted—not by accident, but by design. Books vanished. Teachers fled. Metal detectors replaced music programs. Dreams were stripped down to survival.

Clinics closed. Grocery stores disappeared. Banks abandoned us. In their place came liquor stores, fast food chains, and payday lenders with neon lights and predatory rates. They fed us poison and then blamed us for getting sick.

And while they denied us everything, the headlines said, "This area is struggling." As if neighborhoods self-destruct. As if poverty is pathology. As if we were the problem, not the policies that starved us.

We were not struggling by choice. We were being starved—of resources, of investment, of opportunity, and of dignity. Still, we made something from nothing. We threw block parties under flickering lights. We turned vacant lots into courts and classrooms. We walked our babies past boarded buildings and still called them brilliant—because they were.

But let's be clear: this was not resilience by choice. It was survival by necessity. We weren't born with bootstraps. We were born on battlefields. And they expected us to bloom where they had poisoned the ground.

They didn't just abandon our neighborhoods—they orchestrated their decay. They didn't just forget us—they engineered our failure. And just as despair set in, they returned with plans, permits, and bulldozers, cloaked as rescuers.

They called it "public housing." We knew it as the new plantation. High-rises stacked like tombs, built not to lift us up, but to lock us in. One way in, one way out. Narrow halls. Caged windows. Watchtower balconies. It wasn't oversight—it was surveillance—not support, but control.

And then came the venom, slowly released into the veins of our communities. The drugs didn't grow from our gardens; they were delivered. The guns didn't come from our pockets; they were planted. Addiction spread. Violence followed. And funerals for the young and innocent became heartbreakingly common—normalized in a nation that refused to see the cost of its policies.

This was not a failure of policy—it was the execution of a plan. It was never about *urban renewal*; it was always *urban removal*. A quiet genocide cloaked in government aid, waged not with bombs, but with blueprints. They didn't attack with soldiers, but with systems. They didn't just construct housing projects—they projected pain. And that pain was etched into the very skyline of our cities.

Today, the strategies wear new names—"revitalization, opportunity zones, and affordable housing initiatives"—but the spirit behind them remains the same. The vocabulary has evolved, but the outcome is all too familiar: displacement masquerading as development, gentrification disguised as progress. This is what they now call "turning blight into billions."

The communities that once bore the brunt of disinvestment are now being targeted for profit—not restoration. They come bearing promises of mixed-income housing, but the "mix" seldom includes the people who lived there before the ribbon-cutting. Rents skyrocket. Culture erodes. The soul of the neighborhood—the people—is pushed out, priced out, and written out. And yet, they have the audacity to call it equity.

But God sees. And history speaks louder than the polished brochures. What they call "policy," we recognize as prophecy fulfilled—a divine warning to a nation that continues to build its future on the ruins of the oppressed.

They want us to believe that these stories are isolated, that what happened to one neighborhood was just an unfortunate side effect of progress. But when you map the wounds across this country, a pattern emerges. A trail of blood, bulldozers, and broken promises so clear that even the blind could trace it.

Consider Vine City in Atlanta—the metropolitan area where I grew up. Once a thriving, tight-knit Black community just west of downtown, it was home to civil rights leaders, educators, entrepreneurs, and families who built without permission. But when city leaders decided they needed stadiums, interstates, and parking lots, Vine City was gutted. Homes were bulldozed. Streets were split apart. Families were scattered under the blade of eminent domain.

And when Morris Brown College—the only historically Black college in Atlanta founded by Black people—came under federal investigation, we all knew what was coming. That land was too valuable. Today, where Black dreams once stood, shiny arenas rise in their place. They call it progress. We know it as erasure.

Then look at Black Bottom in Detroit—a heartbeat of Black brilliance. Businesses thrived, music pulsed through the streets, and families defied the odds to build wealth. But then came "renewal." Bulldozers leveled the community. Freeways replaced the families. They paved over excellence and called it economic growth.

Consider Rondo in St. Paul—a neighborhood once bursting with culture, pride, and resilience. That is, until Interstate 94 was built. The highway wasn't constructed around the community or beside it—it was driven straight through it, like a blade slicing through a living, breathing body. It didn't just connect cities; it severed generations. And to this day, the wounds still ache.

These were not accidents, and they were not isolated. They were carefully coordinated campaigns to disrupt and displace Black life. They were acts of war—legislated, funded, and executed in the name of development.

Even now, the new architects of displacement hide behind sophisticated language. They speak of "investment," "revitalization," and "growth." But no luxury condo can cover the blood embedded in the foundation. No entertainment district can drown out the silence where songs once rose from porches and sanctuaries. No economic initiative can undo the theft stretching across generations.

So, what now?

We will not be pacified by symbolic gestures. We will not be comforted by murals painted over pain or museums built atop demolished homes. Our memories are not for sale. Our inheritance is not negotiable. And our communities are not collateral.

We demand repair. Repair is not charity. It is justice delayed. It is a debt owed. It is the minimum reasonable response to a mountain of *compounded theft.*

We demand restitution—not empty apologies spoken from podiums, but tangible, measurable returns. The restitution we demand is direct investment into Black-owned businesses; land trusts to protect the remaining spaces we call home; financial compensation for the generational wealth that was stolen through redlining, blockbusting, and urban renewal; and legal protections to guard against future displacements masked as "development."

We demand equity. We are not looking for gestures of goodwill, but as a righteous reckoning with the destruction engineered into Black communities by white America. Equity means repair. It means returning land, capital, profits earned and contracts to the very neighborhoods that were robbed of them. Equity means a return on our investment. It means access not only to the table, but to ownership of the table—where decisions are made and futures are forged.

We demand rebuilding. Rebuilding on our terms, with our hands, and with our vision. Because they buried us thinking we were seeds they could kill. But seeds buried in injustice grow roots of resistance.

Justice is not a suggestion; it is a command from heaven. The God who watches over the oppressed is calling this nation to account. And if the cries of the enslaved still echo in the soil, then let the roar of their descendants shake the foundations until "justice rolls down like waters, and righteousness like a mighty stream." (Amos 5:24 KJV)

We are not waiting for permission. We are not waiting for validation. We are not just surviving this system. *We are dismantling it.* And what they once called blight, we now call banner.

They built borders to box us in—to fence in our futures and partition our power. But what happens when the people once bound by lines—legal, political, and spiritual— that those lines no longer hold authority?

The uprising does not stop at boundaries. It crosses them. This is the next battleground. Welcome to *Borders*.

8

BORDERS

*"For I was hungry, and you gave me nothing to eat, I was thirsty,
and you gave me nothing to drink, I was a stranger, and you
did not invite me in, I needed clothes, and you did not clothe
me, I was sick and in prison, and you did not look after me."*

MATTHEW 25:42-43 NIV

America is a country built on boundaries—not only national ones, but also racial, social, economic, and spiritual. These borders are not always constructed with bricks. Sometimes they are drawn with bullets. Sometimes they are traced in silence. Other times, they are signed in blood. These lines have been carved through cities, through families, and through futures.

They told us where we could live, where we could walk, and where and when we could learn. They even dared to dictate where we could worship and where we were allowed to simply exist. And when we crossed those lines—when we stepped into spaces they claimed were not ours—they responded with violence.

Ask the child who integrated a school and had to walk through a crowd that spat on her simply for showing up to learn. Ask the man who tried to vote but was met not with a ballot, but with a rope. Ask the woman who dared to preach the gospel when the world told her that she should only pray in silence. Ask the dreamer who tried to build beyond the limits of his neighborhood, only to be greeted with flames instead of celebration.

These lines were never just about geography. They were always about power, about fear, and about control.

Redlining was never just about mortgages. It was a message: *Stay in your place.* Segregation was never just about water fountains. It was a warning: *Don't cross over.* And when those lines failed to keep us out, they drew new ones—this time inside our minds.

They called it zoning. They called it safety. They called it policy. But it was always about territory—about controlling which spaces Black life was permitted to flourish in, and which spaces would punish us for trying to enter. Still, we crossed anyway.

We crossed because we knew something they didn't: what they called forbidden, we called promised. What they called boundaries, we saw as barriers meant to be broken. And every time we stepped over a line drawn in blood, we declared to the systems behind it: *You don't own us. You don't define us. You don't get the final word.*

But some of the most difficult borders we have had to cross aren't drawn on maps—they are drawn on hearts. Not all chains are visible; some are forged in the mind and bound by fear. Not all cages are made of iron; some are built from silence, shame, and unhealed wounds. Not all boundaries were imposed by others; some we built ourselves, out of survival, and then forgot how to tear them down.

There is a border we inherited. A line passed down by generations doing their best to survive a world that hunted them. It was a line that said: *Don't go too far. Don't speak too loudly. Don't dream too big. Don't love too freely. Don't challenge too boldly.* And when we tried to cross it, it was often our own people who pulled us back—not out of hate, but out of fear.

That fear was passed down like a family Bible—worn with use, recited without question, and trusted as truth. It was given not in malice, but in love shaped by trauma. They had seen what happened to those who stepped out of line, and they didn't want that suffering to follow us.

So, protection became a prison. Wisdom became a warning. Survival became silence.

We learned to shrink in broad daylight. We were taught to fold our brilliance into something more "acceptable"—something easier for others to digest. We were told to temper our voices, to measure every word so we wouldn't seem too bold, too loud, or too much. We were told to wear our dignity like armor—quiet, polished, and unthreatening—so it would not provoke fear or resistance.

We learned how to edit our voices in the boardroom. We were taught how to dilute our rage in the sanctuary, to make it sound more like reverence than resistance. We learned how to shape our truth into something softer—how to make it sound like a question, just in case it made someone uncomfortable. Because crossing the border wasn't just about place. It was about *permission.*

Who gave them the right to lead with that kind of authority and conviction? Who told them that they could speak with such clarity and such fire, as if their voice mattered? Who gave them permission to stand as though they knew—without apology—that they are chosen?

We learned to shrink ourselves and call it humility. We were taught to mistake silence for grace and limitation for virtue. But what really shook them to their core was our anointing. What they really feared was what would happen if we ever believed God's Word more than the world's warnings. Because once we cross that inner border—once we tear down the mental maps that say, *"stay small,"* we become unstoppable. We become a holy trespasser. We become a spiritual outlaw.

We become prophets who no longer need other people's platforms because we carry our own altar wherever we go. And when we stop waiting for permission to exist—when we realize that the Kingdom of God has no caste system and walks fully in the authority God has given to us, not the limited version others tried to allow—then every boundary breaks. Because freedom doesn't just show up in systems. It shows up in souls. And the most dangerous rebellion we will ever wage is the one where we reclaim our *own minds*.

America loves borders. It loves building them. It loves defending them. And it loves weaponizing them—especially when they're drawn against Black and brown bodies.

This nation was born from stolen land and fenced in with stolen labor. And it has spent centuries policing the gates of power while pretending they were protecting freedom.

Let's tell the truth: *Borders in America have never been about safety. They've been about supremacy.* They were designed not just to define land, but to deny access.

We have seen borders drawn not only on maps, but across skin tones, surnames, and sacred histories. These were not just physical lines. They were racial boundaries—constructed to control who is seen as worthy, as human, or as belonging. They were not merely immigration checkpoints, but spiritual no-fly zones—spaces where certain bodies, certain languages, and certain lineages were deemed too foreign, too poor, and too dark to pass through.

But we are here now. We carry the passport of divine authority. And we are crossing every border they built to keep us out—with truth in our mouths, legacy in our bones, and the kingdom in our stride.

They say, "Build the wall," as if walls are new. But the truth is, walls have always existed—just not always made of stone. There were walls when redlining carved the suburbs away from the hood, when Black families were boxed out of opportunity with invisible ink on mortgage maps. There are walls now, in the form of immigration detention centers and surveillance drones that police borders not just of nations, but of skin. From the

Berlin Wall that once split a city in two, to the steel barriers rising along the U.S.-Mexico border today—walls have always been less about safety and more about control. They divide who gets to belong from who gets watched, and who gets welcome from who gets warned.

Black people in America were never immigrants. We were cargo.

We didn't cross borders—they crossed us. And yet we're still treated like outsiders on soil soaked with our ancestors' blood.

They built a nation with our hands and still ask for our papers. They birthed their economy from our backs and still question if we belong.

And now, when Black immigrants come—from Haiti, from Nigeria, from Jamaica, or from the continent that mothered the world—they are met with the same border mentality: *"You're too loud. You're too proud. You don't belong here either."*

The boats we came on weren't cruise ships. The shores we landed on weren't welcoming. The documents they demand today are written in the same ink as the slave codes they used yesterday.

Citizenship has always been conditional— It was conditioned on whiteness, on wealth, and on silence. Because they know once we cross that line—once we claim space without apology, once we see that the Kingdom has no borders, once we unite across languages, nations, and bloodlines—*their fences fall.*

We were never meant to simply assimilate into a system that was never built with us in mind. We were called to liberate—to remind a nation obsessed with building walls that God never constructed one. We were sent to declare that every border drawn in hatred is already unlawful in the courts of heaven. We were chosen to show that the gospel was never gated, never nationalized, and never colonized—only corrupted by those who feared it might set too many people free.

And now we see the border for what it is: A line drawn in sand by men who think God honors their politics. But God's justice doesn't need a passport, and His deliverance doesn't stop at customs. Because now that the Kingdom is here, every wall must fall, every gate must swing open, and every captive must walk free.

They didn't just steal land. They stole what the land meant to us. They denied us not only space, but sanctuary.

They carved out neighborhoods where we were allowed to live but never allowed to rest. They allowed our bodies to labor but not to linger in peace.

They gave us sidewalks, but never safety. They allowed us to worship in their churches but stripped us of any power. They gave us houses but denied us a true sense of home. Because what they feared more than our presence was our possession—our ownership, our authority, and our spiritual right to claim what God had already declared as ours.

We know that sacred territory is not always made of soil. Sometimes it is time—time that was stolen. Sometimes it is breath—holy and withheld. And sometimes, sacred territory is simply the right to be still and not be hunted.

But how can you rest in a land where your mere presence is policed? How can you call a space sacred when your prayer meetings are watched, when your children's laughter is mistaken for a threat, and when your mourning is met with arrest?

We have been denied access to stillness—the sacred kind that allows the soul to breathe. We have been denied access to joy, as though it were a luxury we had no right to feel. We have been denied autonomy, our right to move freely, to choose, and to exist without surveillance or suspicion. And we have been denied holy ground, as if the presence of God could be fenced off from us or could only be ushered in at their direction.

They made our neighborhoods battlegrounds, then asked why we couldn't find peace. They turned our schools into prison pipelines, then asked why we weren't graduating. They labeled our faith "too emotional," our worship "too wild," and our theology "too dangerous"—because we dared to see ourselves in Scripture not as footnotes, but as freedom fighters.

They told us our churches were "too political" because we preached Exodus while they built Egypt. But we know what's sacred. We know what it means to anoint street corners with oil and scripture. We know what it means to cast out spirits that wear uniforms and policies. We know what it means to claim land that was labeled cursed—and call it holy because we're still here.

They denied us sacred territory. So we made it ourselves. We turned stoops into sanctuaries. We transformed block parties into revivals. We changed cell blocks into testimonies and grief into gospel. Because anywhere God walks with us is holy. And He has been walking with us through every border they ever built.

So now we declare: This *territory* is sanctified. This *presence* is prophetic. These *people* are unstoppable. And we will no longer ask for access to what we already carry within.

Every time we crossed a line they drew for us, we didn't just survive—we shattered the lie that tried to contain us. Because we were never meant to stay inside their boxes.

We were not meant for the housing projects or the back pews. The "diversity hire" seat at someone else's table wasn't meant for us. And the labels—"angry," "urban," "too loud," and "too much" were not ours, either.

We were never too much. They just gave us too little. And when we refused to shrink, when we stepped over the thresholds they guarded with laws, guns, and silence—we became dangerous. It wasn't because we had weapons, but because we had vision.

Black girls defying the odds and enrolling in colleges their grandmothers could only clean. Black men standing in pulpits without permission. Black mothers starting businesses in kitchens where nothing was promised but grit and grace. Black students refusing to edit their brilliance just to be palatable. Black immigrants building empires from scratch while the system dared them to fail.

That is what crossing the line looks like. Every time we speak in rooms they never imagined us in, we're crossing the line. Every time we name injustice in a language they tried to silence—we're crossing the line. Every time we believe God's promises over a country's restrictions—we're crossing the line. And when we cross, we don't apologize. We don't ask for permission. We plant a flag. Because we know we don't just belong in those spaces—we're called to transform them.

We are not here to assimilate into systems that were never meant to sustain us. We are here to uproot old ideologies and to plant seeds of regeneration that bear justice, truth, and hope. We are here to reimagine what the world can be.

We are here to turn courtrooms into confessionals—places where truth is told and healing begins. We are here to turn classrooms into launchpads where young minds are equipped, not confined. We are here to turn neighborhoods into nations—strong, sovereign, and self-determined.

We are here to turn *ghettos into goldmines*, uncovering the buried brilliance within our communities. We are here to turn *history into healing*—not by forgetting the past, but by confronting it with courage.

They will call it rebellion. We will call it restoration. We are not just crossing borders. We are creating a new geography.

The maps they drew are lies. They were lines built on fear. They are districts carved out of greed. They are neighborhoods labeled to control what could be grown there—and who could *never* rise there. But we were never called to live according to their geography. This land is not what the deed says. It is what the Spirit declares.

We are mapping something new. We are not redrawing the lines with their rulers and compasses—we are redrawing them with our memory, our presence, and our power. We map this moment not according to their measurements, but according to the truth we carry in our bones. Because what we build now is not shaped by conquest—it is shaped by covenant.

The block they called "at risk"—we now call it *anointed*. The house they boarded up—we call it *blessed*. The street they said was "unsafe"— we call it *our sanctuary*. Because geography has never just been about land. It's about what we make of it.

They labeled our communities by crime rate. We measured them by community. We assess them by cookouts, by choirs, by cornerstones, and by communion.

They defined space by profit. We define it by *presence*. The presence of people who refuse to leave. The presence of prayer that refuses to be silenced. The presence of ancestors who never got to see the fruit but sowed the seed anyway.

This is the new geography. Where power isn't concentrated at the top— it's poured out on the overlooked. Where healing doesn't come from the city—it comes from the soil. Where we don't just demand access to space— we *consecrate* it.

A classroom becomes a sanctuary. A barbershop becomes a think tank. A stoop becomes a war room. A sanctuary becomes a command center.

We're not just reclaiming territory. We're transforming it. And we won't stop at our blocks.

We are coming for the boardrooms—to claim seats at tables where decisions are made about our future. We are coming for the ballots—to exercise the power our ancestors bled for and to shape policy with purpose. We are coming for the budgets—to direct the flow of resources toward justice, equity, and restoration. We are coming for the blueprints—to redesign what was built to exclude us and to construct what reflects who we truly are.

And in every space we step into, we sanctify it—not with permission, but with presence. We fill it with truth. We flood it with joy. We anchor it in power—not because they allowed it, but because God already declared it.

This isn't gentrification. It's glorification.

We are launching a holy invasion into every place they said we didn't belong. We are stepping into spaces that once shut us out—because our presence is prophetic. We go not in rebellion, but in righteousness. Because the Kingdom of God does not recognize the borders they drew in fear, in greed, or in hate. And we do not honor them either.

We move with divine authority, not institutional approval. We cross every man-made line with the confidence that heaven has already cleared the way.

We've crossed the lines. We've reclaimed the ground. We've redefined the map. And now, we stand—not as exiles, but as heirs.

This is not the kind of exodus they wrote about in textbooks—where escape was the only option. This is not the old story of running away. This is the Exodus that stayed. We stayed in neighborhoods marked for erasure, where developers saw only profit, but we saw legacy. We stayed on the land our ancestors tilled with broken backs and unbreakable spirits. We stayed in cities that never wanted us but could never get rid us—no matter how hard they tried. We stayed and declared, "This time, we're not leaving. This time, we're leading." Because deliverance doesn't always look like escape. Sometimes, it looks like standing your ground—and reclaiming it.

What happens when we—the people who were always expected to disappear—decide not to vanish, but to dig in? What shifts when we choose to stay, to build, and to plant generational roots where they hoped we'd never rise? We confront the Pharaohs of today—not with plagues, but with policy shaped by wisdom, with prayer fueled by fire, and with presence that refuses to be ignored.

We are no longer asking for space. We are occupying it—with purpose, with power, and with the authority of those who know they were never meant to be erased.

This Exodus is not about getting out—it is about taking over. We were not delivered just to escape; we were anointed to inherit. We are becoming the landlords of the very land they told us we would never own. We are turning captivity into covenant and transforming stolen labor into sacred legacy. We are flipping the narrative—so that the oppressed are no longer survivors alone, but the architects of what comes next.

We did not cross all these borders, bear all this pain, and endure all this history just to leave again. We crossed to plant roots that cannot be uprooted. We crossed to plant flags that mark territory claimed by justice. We crossed to plant futures—generational, unapologetic, and unstoppable.

We are the deliverance we've been waiting for. And now, the soil beneath our feet? It is not just land. It is legacy. It is holy.

We write books, make films, curate art, and tell our stories in our own voices—not as side notes to whitewashed history, but as the center of truth. Every time we speak our ancestors' names with honor, every time we challenge a lie with lived experience, we break chains of silence and empower future generations to rise to their calling.

Let the Pharaohs tremble. Let the gates rattle. Let the systems take notice: the Exodus has arrived. But this time, we are not running—we are rising. We have planted ourselves in the rubble. We have built altars out of ashes. We have laid claim to the land they tried to fence off with fear.

We understand now that staying is not the end of deliverance. Because once we reclaim what was taken, we must ask the sacred question: *What will we build?*

And now, we build bridges. Not to make peace with oppression, but to carve a path through the wreckage it left behind. Not to smooth over injustice, but to stretch our legacy across every divide they told us could not be crossed.

For too long, they have built walls—Walls between races and generations. Walls between power and the people. Walls between heaven and earth. Walls between the ones who left and the ones who stayed. Walls between the pulpit and the street, between the church and the culture, between the truth and the telling of it.

But we are the generation that will not be walled in. We are the ones who rise not to escape but to establish. And what we build now—will last.

But this generation? We're not wall-builders. We are bridge-bearers.

We are the ones who stay rooted and still reach. We are the ones who know how to hold memory in one hand and mercy in the other. We are the ones who walk into fractured spaces and don't choose a side—we create a way. Because real deliverance isn't just about escape.

It's about elevation. It's about connection. It's about building something better than what broke us.

This is the moment where the Exodus becomes a movement. This is where rebellion is no longer just resistance—it becomes restoration. We are no longer surviving the separation; we are walking boldly into reconciliation. But not the kind of reconciliation that demands our silence or forgetfulness. We are stepping into the kind that remembers the wounds, honors the struggle, and redeems the story.

We are not here to erase the past—we are here to heal it. And in that healing, we are building a future rooted in justice, soaked in truth, and crowned with glory.

This is the next chapter.

Bridges, not walls. Because the only thing stronger than what divided us is the people willing to reach across it anyway.

9

BRIDGES,
NOT WALLS

"We build too many walls and not enough bridges."

ISAAC NEWTON

A merica has always been a country built on walls—brick, legal, theological, and psychological. These walls determine who is included and who is excluded. They draw the lines between those deemed safe and those labeled suspect. They define who belongs and who had better not knock too loudly.

Walls don't just divide—they define. The plantation was a wall. It separated the enslaved from the owners, the field from the house, the human from the rights.

The Mason-Dixon line was a wall. It was a line that tried to split morality in half and call it compromise.

Jim Crow was a wall. It was built in courts, churches, lunch counters, water fountains, and bathrooms.

Mass incarceration is a wall. It is still standing. It's still swallowing generations whole.

Even now, our neighborhoods remain divided by highways. Our schools are separated by zip codes. Our politics are driven by fear. Our churches remain fractured by silence. And for every wall that was built, a name was assigned to justify it—Order, Law, Safety, Tradition, Theology. But what was truly constructed was distance. And distance always comes at a cost.

Love cannot exist without proximity. Healing cannot happen without listening. Change cannot come without the courage to confront what stands in the way.

Walls have built legacies of mistrust. They have built legacies of loss, of ignorance, and of systems deliberately designed to keep people strangers in the same land. For generations, these walls were justified as measures of protection. But walls do not protect—they prevent.

They prevent reconciliation. They prevent accountability. They prevent communion.

Walls do not simply divide bodies; they separate souls. They do not only block physical movement; they block meaning. They block memory. They block the miracle of being seen. And when a wall stands long enough, people begin to forget there was ever a bridge in its place.

This is the toll of separation. It is not always loud or dramatic. Sometimes, it is silent. Sometimes, it lingers like tension in the air—unspoken, unnamed—but felt every time a room is entered.

It reveals itself in the side-eyes exchanged across crowded rooms. It lingers in the heavy sighs that carry generations of weariness. It shows up in the reluctance to trust, in the guarded posture that protects what little space is believed to be owned.

It was present in the atmosphere that Saturday. It was an unspoken weight that could be felt more than explained.

I went to Costco—my usual weekly shopping trip—but something in the air was off. It was crowded, tense, and I was alone. My son was traveling, and his absence made the weight of everything feel heavier—more raw.

Since Donald Trump's re-election, it had been building. This invisible weight, this sharp edge was hanging in the air.

Kindness had become scarce, and compassion was increasingly viewed as a weakness. A "push and shove" mentality seemed to dominate every space. It was no longer just about getting ahead; it was also about ensuring someone else did not.

This raised a pressing question: Can one individual change the atmosphere overnight? Or did that individual simply give others permission to unleash what had long been buried within?

I was already pacing myself, careful not to draw too much attention as I made my way through the crowded parking lot. I didn't want to outpace anyone. I was just trying to make it through the chaos with my groceries and get home. But then came the moment that changed everything.

I had motioned to a young woman—another shopper—that I was pulling out of a parking space so she could have it. It was simple. It was kind. Or at least, that's what I thought.

But before I could back out, an Indian woman pulled up and turned on her blinker. She saw me communicating with the other woman and immediately erupted.

"You can't decide who gets your parking space!" she shouted. Then, from her window came the words I never expected to hear: "You Black b— you can't do that!"

I froze. There we were—two women of color, two strangers—and suddenly, I found myself in the crosshairs of someone else's assumption, someone else's anger, someone else's wall.

It wasn't just about a parking space. It was about how quickly we've turned on each other. About how deeply suspicion and scarcity have carved rifts between us. About how easily pain, left unchecked, can make us territorial, petty, and even cruel.

And in that moment, I let it affect me. My heart began to race. Heat rushed through my body in a way I rarely experience. I realized I had crossed an invisible threshold—from routine to rage, from safety to sorrow—in the span of mere seconds.

As I hurried to return my cart to the corral, I noticed an Asian man and his wife doing the same. He looked up. Our eyes met. And in that brief, unspoken moment, something holy passed between us.

He didn't say a word. But I saw the confusion in his eyes. I saw the compassion. It was as if he, too, was trying to make sense of what we had just witnessed—two strangers, both women of color, carrying the weight of too many unspoken walls, colliding in the parking lot of a grocery store.

That is the toll. We have become so accustomed to division that we no longer know how to connect. So conditioned by competition, we have forgotten how to care. So deeply shaped by trauma, we misinterpret even the gentlest intentions.

We have reached a place where even the sharing of a parking space can trigger a sense of being unseen, disrespected, or left behind. But peace does not have to come at someone else's expense. And bridges are not built through suspicion. They are built through healing.

Time alone does not heal all wounds. But love does. Forgiveness does. Compassion—especially the kind that dares to reach across race, across pain, across misunderstanding—that heals.

We do not excuse hatred. But we refuse to be shaped by it. Because the toll of separation has been too high. And we have already paid enough.

Now, it is time to build. We build with every gesture of grace. With every conversation that begins with, "I see you." With every apology that becomes restoration. With every moment we choose presence over pride, we establish a better world for all of us.

Because the enemy's greatest lie is that we are each other's competition. But the truth is this: when we are united, we are unstoppable.

Walls isolate. Bridges unite. And love builds what pain tried to tear down. We are done living behind walls.

This is the chapter where we begin to name the walls—so that we can begin to tear them down. Brick by brick. Lie by lie. Fear by fear. Because before we can build the bridge, we must face what built the wall.

Before there were policies, there were people. Before the world spoke of equity, there were mothers praying through the night. There were fathers swallowing their pride to provide. There were neighbors watching each other's children like they were their own. Before any program, there was always a person who stood up and said, "Not on my watch."

Bridge builders are not always loud. They do not always hold microphones or megaphones. They often carry grief in one hand and grace in the other. They walk the sacred ground between conflict and compassion, between the past and the possible, between what hurt us and what can heal us.

Bridge builders stood in the middle—when it wasn't safe. They forgave before the other side ever said, "Sorry." They showed up in rooms where they weren't welcome—not to fit in, but to make room for someone else.

Bridge building is holy work. It is legacy work. It is what Harriet did. What Dr. King did. What every protestor with sore feet and righteous fury has done.

It's what that Asian man did in the Costco parking lot when his eyes met mine. He didn't have a verse to quote or a speech to give. But in one moment of shared humanity, he stepped into the wreckage of my pain and, with his presence, said, "I see you."

That was the beginning of a bridge. Not one built with brick or steel, but with an open heart and a steady gaze.

Bridge builders walk slow. Not because they are weak, but because they are carrying something sacred. They carry the memory of pain and the weight of possibility. They have seen both sides of the wall and still believe in connection.

They are not idealists. They are intercessors. They are the answer to someone's desperate prayer for peace. They are the reason some of us didn't quit. They are the reason healing is still possible. And some of them are us.

We have built bridges with our silence when we could have retaliated. With our endurance when others tried to erase us. With our truth when the world begged us to lie just to keep the peace.

And now it's time to say it plainly: Bridge builders are warriors. Bridge builders are prophets. Bridge builders are revolutionaries.

What takes more strength—to build a wall to keep people out, or to build a bridge wide enough for your enemy to walk across and become your brother?

You don't build a bridge on untouched ground. You build it over a gap, over a gash, over the places where something split—hard, fast, and deep.

We don't get to skip the wound. We build over it—not to cover it up, but to honor it. To ensure that the next traveler doesn't fall into what almost swallowed us whole.

The plantation was a wound. We heal it by building over it with land ownership, legacy, and liberation.

The Mason-Dixon Line was a wound. We heal it by building relationships that cross state lines, class lines, and skin.

Jim Crow was a wound. We heal it with equity, education, and systems designed to serve—not segregate.

Mass incarceration is a wound. We heal it with policy reform, reentry support, prison abolition, reinstatement of voting rights, and sacred advocacy.

These walls broke bodies. Our bridges restore breath.

This is not about forgetting what was done. It is about walking back into the wreckage with tools in our hands. Because the only thing holy enough to cover a wound is not shame—it is structure. It is purpose. It is presence.

A bridge is not just about getting from one side to the other. It is about saying, "You don't get to define what this space means anymore."

The middle ground—where the wound lives—becomes the place of transformation. It is the place where we take what the enemy meant for evil and allow God to turn it for our good and His glory.

Our God, who is Love, redeems us right in the place where the lash once split skin. And now, where there was once blood, there is a lavish garden.

Where the iron bars once stole time, now we build futures. Where policy once choked possibility, now we write new legislation—with new names and sacred intentions.

We are the architects of resurrection. We do not build because we are fully healed. We build because we are healing. We do not build because it is easy. We build because the next generation should not have to climb the same walls we did just to breathe.

And if we do it right—they won't even know there was once a wound beneath the bridge. They will simply walk across what we made in love and call it home.

Not all bridges are made of steel and stone. Some are built from grace. Not the kind that excuses injustice, but the kind that holds the weight of history and still chooses to heal anyway.

This is the architecture of grace. It starts with truth—not denial, and not revision. Without truth, there is no foundation strong enough to bear the weight.

You cannot build connection on a lie. You cannot reach across pain if you refuse to name it.

Then comes justice—not vengeance, but alignment. Grace is not grace if it does not confront. Justice is the beam that stretches across the gap. It dares to say, "We will not repeat this again."

Next comes mercy—not forgetting but forgiving. Not letting go of memory but letting go of bitterness. Mercy is the space between the planks—flexible, not fragile. It bends with the winds of struggle. It sways under the weight of tension. But it holds.

And finally, there is love. Not sentiment—but strategy. Love that builds wide enough for all of us. Love that refuses to create "us vs. them." Love that builds bridges, even when the person on the other side voted against our freedom.

This is holy engineering. You don't build it alone. You don't build it fast. You don't build it for applause.

You build it for the crossing—for the person too tired to fight. For the elder who never saw healing in their lifetime. For the child who doesn't yet know the names of the walls we've torn down so they could run freely.

Because the most powerful bridges are not built in victory. They are built in faith.

They are built when people on both sides aren't sure if they're ready—but they come anyway. They come not to surrender, but to stand—together.

Because grace is not weakness. Grace is architecture. And when it is built right, it will hold for generations.

Let them build their walls. Let them stack their bricks of fear, policy, and pride. Let them fortify their privilege and dig moats around their comfort. Because while they build walls—we will build bridges.

They build to divide. We build to connect. They build for protection. We build for possibility. They build for power. We build for people.

Because the walls were never truly about keeping danger out. They were about keeping transformation from getting in. They are terrified of what happens when those on the other side of the wall realize they were never the problem—but the solution.

So we keep building. We build across generations so grandmothers and granddaughters can heal together. We build across cultures because the Kingdom of God has never been one color, one language, or one zip code. We build across class, across denominations, across past political harm and present spiritual hope.

And every bridge we build is an act of resistance. The world expects us to hate each other. To stay in our corners. To war from our trenches.

But bridges turn enemies into neighbors. Bridges dismantle echo chambers. Bridges make space for the Spirit to move—uncontained.

This is the strategy of the Kingdom of God: not walls, but wounds turned into walkways. Scars turned into stories. Testimonies turned into timber.

We are not naive. We know some will never cross. Some will cling to their walls of fear, supremacy, and shame.

But while they isolate, we multiply. We will outlast the wall because we will out love it. We will out serve it. We will outdream it.

Let them build what they want. Let headlines declare division. Let systems try to separate what God is bringing together. For the Word declares, "What God has joined together, let no man—or woman—separate." That is not just about marriage. That is about covenant.

And for every wall they raise, there will be a people with vision, nails, and holy ambition, building something stronger.

Bridges—not walls. Unity—not uniformity. Grace—not gatekeeping. Let the bridge be wide. Let the welcome be radical. Let the crossing begin.

We have crossed borders. We have built bridges over the ruins they left behind. We have made sanctuaries in the gaps, altars in the alleys, and peace in places where pain once had the loudest voice. But the bridge was never the destination. It was the path. And now that we have crossed it— we must confront the flag.

Because the bridge leads straight to the doorstep of a question that has burned for centuries in the bodies of the overlooked: Is there room for us—truly—for the brown, the Black, the Native, the immigrant, the displaced—in the red, white, and blue? Is there room in a country that was built on our backs but breaks itself at the thought of our full inclusion?

We are not just bridge-builders. We are fire-carriers. We are carriers of memory, of resistance, and of holy unrest. We carry the fire of those who marched long before the cameras ever showed up. We carry the fire of those who bled before there were hashtags to bear witness. We carry the fire of those who preached deliverance in churches that doubled as shelters, offering both sanctuary and strategy. We carry the fire of those who taught children how to read freedom between the lines of books that never even spoke their names. We carry fire—not to burn down what remains, but to expose what is still hiding. Because the flag may wave, but does it welcome? It sings of liberty, but does it listen?

We are not asking to be tolerated. We are asking whether this nation can look itself in the mirror and tell the truth about who it really belongs to. And we ask—not with bitterness—but with fire.

It is the fire of a people who have carried this country forward, even while it tried to drag us back. It is the fire of faith—faith forged in the crucible of slavery, ignited through protest, and sustained by the power of the Spirit.

So, we ask, plainly, painfully, prophetically: Is there room for brown in the red, white, and blue? Because even if the answer is no—we will still carry the fire. We will still build. We will still rise. And the day will come when what they refused to make room for will become the very light that shows them the way.

ANY ROOM FOR BROWN IN THE RED, WHITE, AND BLUE?

They say, "This land is your land. This land is my land."

Being brown in America has always meant navigating an uneasy landscape—one layered with contradictions, exclusions, and silent expectations. It is to live in a place shaped by the work of our hands but rarely designed with our flourishing in mind.

It means walking through a nation that celebrates freedom loudly, yet so often stifles the freedom of those who don't fit the mold it silently constructed. It means entering houses our ancestors built brick by brick, only to be greeted at the threshold with suspicion, hesitation, or the demand to shrink. It feels like preparing the feast, seasoning every dish, serving each plate, and then being asked to wait outside while others eat.

It means our celebrations are often tokenized, our grievances are politicized, and our contributions are contextualized only when they can no longer be ignored. Praise greets us when we entertain, discomfort when we speak truth, and silence when we mourn openly. And through it all, we carry the tension of being both essential and excluded.

To walk in brown skin across this country is to bear the invisible weight of historical erasure and modern denial. Suspicion trails behind our steps, lurking in the glances of strangers, tightening in the clutch of a purse or the resting of a hand on a holster. It means enduring comments like, "Go back to your country," from those unaware—or unwilling to remember—that our ancestors stood on this land long before theirs ever arrived.

It means knowing that our labor built more than cities. Our sweat laid down tracks that connected commerce across regions, paved roads that others travel freely, harvested crops that filled markets, and stitched garments worn proudly by a nation that still asks us for credentials.

We remember the Little Rock Nine who needed the National Guard to walk into school. We remember Sylvia Mendez, whose case paved the way for desegregating schools in California, years before Brown v. Board of Education. We remember Japanese American families forced into internment camps; their loyalty questioned as their property was seized. We remember Chinese families separated for decades by exclusion laws, and Filipino farm workers who organized for fair wages but were written out of the labor movement's story.

This history is not a distant shadow. It is alive in the present, etched into our family stories, held in the memories of our elders, carried in the marrow of our bones.

To be brown in America often means mastering two dialects: the truth we live and the translation we perform. We soften our accents to be understood. We field questions about our hair, our clothes, our names—questions that, beneath their surface, ask us to justify our presence. We are celebrated for our "diversity" while being asked to leave our difference at the door.

We are encouraged to celebrate the Fourth of July, but if we speak of Juneteenth, we are told it is too political. We are expected to sing the national anthem with pride, even as we remember that our ancestors were left out of the very freedom it proclaims.

We are praised for resilience but punished for resistance. When we grieve aloud, we are labeled angry. When we grieve quietly, we are labeled indifferent. We are too visible to be ignored, but too brown to be fully accepted. Our excellence is expected. Our mistakes are magnified.

We raise our children to be proud, to know their history, to stand tall in rooms that try to shrink them. And still, we worry. We wonder whether pride will be mistaken for arrogance.

Our concern weighs heavily on us as we wonder whether our children's confidence will be misinterpreted as a threat. We question whether their brilliance will be enough to shield them from a system conditioned to see their bodies before recognizing their humanity.

Our days are shaped by a rhythm of resistance and remembrance. We balance righteous anger with holy joy. We carry hope not as naïveté, but as necessity. We make room for ourselves where there was none, constantly calculating how much of our truth is allowed.

We are not the problem. Our brownness is not a blemish. Our culture is not a disruption. Our languages, our songs, our prayers—these are not foreign. They are foundational. They are what kept us whole when policies tried to split us apart.

True belonging was never meant to be transactional. It was never meant to be earned through silence or exchanged for proximity. Belonging should not require payment—especially not when our ancestors' blood watered the very soil of this nation. It should not be conditional when their songs carried through cotton fields and sugarcane rows, echoing hope in the face of suffering. It should not be negotiable when their labor sustained this country through war, economic collapse, and the fragile illusion of Reconstruction.

And yet, America turned belonging into a privilege—one that can be granted or revoked at will. We were told to assimilate but never given a reason why. We were told to be American, but only if we buried our roots deep enough to be invisible. We were expected to speak English, but not Spanglish. To cook our food but not bring its aroma into their break rooms. To share our culture, but only in the fragments that made others feel entertained, not uncomfortable.

We remember the Indian boarding schools that tried to erase language and identity. We remember Operation Wetback, which deported thousands of Mexican Americans—many of whom were citizens. We remember COINTELPRO's[5] targeting of civil rights leaders who dared to dream aloud. We remember how the war on drugs ravaged our neighborhoods, how urban renewal became code for displacement, how public housing was both offered and weaponized.

So when they talk about inclusion, we ask: inclusion into what? Because we have learned that inclusion without transformation is just assimilation with a better PR campaign.

True belonging begins with memory. It begins with the kind of memory that restores dignity to those who have been erased or overlooked. It is the memory that confronts and challenges the sanitized narratives we have been taught to accept. It is the memory that refuses to forget the hands that tilled the soil, the backs that bent under the weight of labor, and the minds that dared to imagine a world more free than the one they inherited.

We are not guests in this story. We are architects of its very structure. We are the steel beams, the keystones, the riverbeds beneath the bridges they now cross.

We are not here to fix broken tables. We are planting our own orchards. In these orchards, truth is the root system. Justice is the water. The fruit is shared, not hoarded. The soil is sacred, not selective.

To belong means no longer apologizing for how we show up. It means standing in rooms and telling our stories as if heaven itself is

5. "discredit, disrupt, and destroy": FBI Records acquired by the library reveal violent surveillance of black leaders, civil rights organizations. UC Berkeley Library. (n.d.). https://www.lib.berkeley.edu/about/news/fbi

listening—because it is. It means living as though freedom did not forget us—because it didn't.

We don't need permission to carry pride in our heritage. We don't need validation from a flag that once flew over stolen land and stolen lives. We carry our own banner. It is stamped in brown, woven with fire, and drenched in survival.

Our names are often mispronounced but never misplaced. Our contributions footnoted, our grief misread, our power underestimated. But still, we endure.

We have fought in every war. We have taught in every institution. We have created, cultivated, and healed. We have built what others benefit from, even when we were denied access to its bounty.

We do not rise because we need to prove anything. We rise because rising is in our bloodline.

This is not a story of superiority. It is a story of sacred presence. It is the understanding that what was once sidelined was always central.

And so, we continue—laboring, leading, learning, lifting, not out of obligation, but out of purpose. We continue not because we need to be accepted, but because we know who we are.

We are not the aftermath of someone else's dream. We are the dream itself. We are the prayer uttered under breath. We are the vision passed from elder to child. We are the story they could not erase.

We move forward not to ask if there is room, but to remind the world that there always was—that we were never additions. We were the origin.

We have never been on the margins. We are the roots. We have never been outsiders. We are the soil. We are not problems to be solved. We are the possibility that was planted long ago—and has never stopped growing.

And now, something is shifting. It's not loud. It's not always visible. But it is steady, like a drumbeat returning to a song long interrupted. We feel it when we gather, when we reclaim space, when we build institutions not because we are tolerated in them, but because we lead them. We sense it in the way we are beginning to tell the truth, not just about what was done to us, but about what we have done to survive, to thrive, and to prophesy something better.

We are no longer just surviving. We are designing. Shaping something new with hands once calloused by chains. We are casting vision in the very language that was once banned from our mouths. We are walking back into stolen land—not to reclaim what was, but to build what must be.

This is the space between. It is the wilderness before the garden, and the valley between Egypt and Canaan. It is where we stretch out our hands, scarred and sacred, and say, "We will not carry these burdens across the Jordan."

We have carried names that were never our own. We have answered to labels that reduced us, stripping away the richness and complexity of who we are. We have worn masks crafted to make others feel comfortable—masks that concealed our truth in exchange for temporary acceptance. But we choose to wear them no longer. We are laying them down, not in surrender, but in preparation. The place we are going requires the fullness of who we are.

We are a generation that both remembers and reimagines. We sing songs that are older than our oppression—songs passed down in defiance and in hope. We are building schools not merely for education, but for liberation. We are drafting legislation with ink that carries both justice and memory. We are calling forth healing, not as spectacle, but as structural policy.

We understand now that freedom is not a destination to be crossed. It is a field to be tended. It is a living story that must be told again and again. It is a song that cannot fall silent. And so, we move forward—not as wanderers searching for a place, but as workers preparing one. Not as exiles from history, but as architects of restoration.

We are learning how to live rooted in love and unafraid of legacy. We are rediscovering the ground beneath our feet—not just as soil, but as sanctuary. We are remembering that we are not the ones who need to beg for belonging. We are the ones who bless the places we enter. We are not seeking to be let in. We are the ones who set the table.

And so the bridge is not just behind us. It is beneath us. Each step forward is a sacred crossing. Each act of courage is a plank laid down. Each truth spoken is a beam of strength. We are walking on what our ancestors prayed for.

What lies ahead is not utopia. It is not free of struggle. But it is holy. It is the land they dreamed of—not just in geography, but in justice. It is a place where freedom is not seasonal. It's a place where memory is not buried but built into the architecture. It is a place where rest is not earned through pain but given through promise.

We are not rushing. We are not dragging our feet. We are walking with intention—toward something sacred, something promised. The ground may still tremble, but our steps are sure.

That is because we are the fire carriers. The ones who crossed bridges and borders. The ones who stayed in the Exodus. The ones who lit the path with holy rage and sacred hope.

If there is still any space remaining in this country's conscience, then that space must be made for us—not as guests who require permission, but as guardians who carry both memory and mandate. We are not present as threats; we are present as truth. We are not here to serve as tokens; we are the living testimony that America has not yet become what it claims to be—but it still holds the potential to fulfill that promise, precisely because we are here.

We asked if there was room. But we never needed their answer because the question wasn't about permission—it was about possession. And now, after the bridges we've built, after the walls we've torn down, and after the fire we've carried through generations of exile and erasure—we arrive at a holy revelation: We are the promise.

We are not searching for a place where we might fit in. Instead, we are claiming the ground that has already been inscribed into our very bones. We are not pursuing the version of America that others imagined; we are stepping into the one our ancestors spoke of in hushed tones—through fields and freedom songs. It is the vision of a land where truth flows freely like water and justice is not reduced to a political slogan but becomes the very way we live.

This is the moment when survival transforms into sovereignty. It is the moment when resistance takes root and becomes grounded. It is the moment when brown feet plant themselves firmly in the soil and proclaim with certainty: "We are no longer wandering. This land belongs to us as well. This is the Promised Land."

It is not a land without struggle, but a land where we don't have to disappear to belong. It is not a land built on someone else's blueprint, but one shaped by faith, by fire, and by the stories they tried to silence.

The Promised Land is not perfect, but it is possible. And it will not be inherited by the loudest voices—it will be inherited by the most faithful builders.

We are no longer asking if we fit in the flag. We are raising our own—stitched with justice, anointed with tears, held up by generations who refused to die with the dream inside them.

So now we cross—not out of Egypt, and not into assimilation but into something sacred—into The Promised Land. This is not just the end of a journey. It is the crossing into the next chapter. This is the path into The Promised Land.

II

THE PROMISED LAND

'Get your provisions ready. Three days from now you will
cross the Jordan here to go in and take possession of the
land the Lord your God is giving you for your own.'"

JOSHUA 1:11

Y ou do not enter the Promised Land clean. You do not arrive here
unscathed. You come carrying both the bruises of bondage and the
breath of new beginning. You walk in not because it was easy, but because
the wilderness dared you to keep going. You are here not because you were
lucky, but because you were faithful. And now the ground beneath your
feet is both sacred and scarred.

I remember when my mother was diagnosed with pancreatic cancer,
she gave me a charge. She didn't have time for long speeches or lectures.
Her body grew thin while mine bore the weight of everything I had consumed to bury my pain—shame, grief, disappointment, all layered in
the form of flesh. I was overweight not just from food, but from forgetting myself. From years of silence and self-sabotage. But my mother—
she saw me. She saw the best in me even as her days were numbered,
and she made a final plea: Live. She wanted me to not just live longer,
but a fuller life.

She told me to lose the weight, but what she really meant was: find yourself. Before I leave, promise me you'll find your way back.

She knew what the doctors had confirmed: her days were limited. But she saw something in me worth preserving. Beneath the extra weight I carried—weight born of years of silent suffering, emotional starvation, and forgotten dreams—she saw life.

I was grossly overweight. It wasn't just the weight in my body, but in my spirit. Overfed by shame. Bloated with neglect. Stuffed with unresolved grief and swallowed self-worth. My mother's plea wasn't just for a slimmer figure. It was for freedom. So I reached out to my brother, a personal trainer, and asked for help. And for the first time in a long time, I helped myself. The pounds began to fall, but more than that, the lies I believed about my worth began to shed.

In six months, I had lost one hundred pounds. I didn't just lose the weight from my frame, but from my future. And for ten years, I kept the weight off. I held that promise like a banner over my life—until the world shut down. The pandemic didn't just invade our lungs. It invaded our habits. By 2022, I saw the scale inching back up, the silent enemy returning. But this time, I was not the same woman. I had walked too far to turn back.

I told myself: I'm not going back. I had touched the edge of the promise, and I refused to retreat. Because the Promised Land is not a place you reach once. It's a place you commit to daily. It doesn't come with trumpets. It comes with tenacity. It doesn't end the war. It changes the terrain.

We think when we get there, it will feel different. We believe that heaven will open, and we will hear angels singing. We envision that our pain will dissolve. But the truth is, arrival isn't a finish line. It's a revelation. We discover that what we thought would end the battle only begins it because the Promised Land still has enemies. It still has weeds. It still has voices that say you don't belong. But you do.

The Promised Land doesn't come gift-wrapped. It comes with *giants still in it*. It comes with weeds in the soil. It comes with people who don't believe you deserve to be here—even though you bled for this ground.

Arrival doesn't mean ease. It means now, you build. It means now, you fight from *within*, not to *get in*. Now, you tend to what you've been entrusted with because this is what they never tell you about the Promised Land: It doesn't erase the wilderness. It requires it.

The promise was never about paradise. It was about purpose. It is a land where the legacy of the oppressed is no longer buried—it becomes the law that governs the future. Where we don't just exist—we establish.

The Promised Land doesn't mean no more conflict. It means you no longer fight as a slave. You fight as an heir with vision in your heart and fire in your bones.

And when you look around—at the blocks we reclaimed, the bridges we built, the borders we crossed, and the scars we now wear like sacred blueprints—you realize: This is what survival was preparing us for.

It was not for us to escape. We are here to receive our inheritance.

We did not come to rest from the fight—we came to find rest within it. We did not arrive to lounge in luxury. We arrived to lay foundations deep enough to last generations. We came to plant what our ancestors never got to harvest. We came to raise our children on land that speaks our language and sings our names back to us with every sunrise.

This is not the end of the journey. This is the beginning—not of ease, but of establishment.

Before we ever laid hands on the promise, we walked through places that tried to kill us. And they failed. That, in itself, was the first miracle.

Because the wilderness was never just a delay—it was a refiner. It stripped us of what could not stay. It tested us until only what was true remained. It pressed us until the lies broke and the light got through.

It was there that we learned to hear God without needing a pulpit. We learned how to lead without applause. We learned how to hope without visible signs. And we learned how to worship—not with material offerings, but with nothing in our hands and fire burning in our chest.

The wilderness taught us discipline. It taught us how to live on daily manna, trusting that what we had for today would be enough. It taught us to follow what we could not track—to move when the cloud moved and to remain still when it did not.

It taught us to discern the difference between an enemy and a familiar form of bondage. It taught us how to recognize the line between a promised battle and a fear-driven retreat. It trained our spirits to distinguish what simply felt good from what was truly of God.

In the wilderness, our idols were shattered. Our false identities were stripped away. The voices we once trusted more than our own were exposed for what they were. And then came the silence—not as punishment, but as an invitation. It was in the stillness that we remembered how to listen again. Because there are some truths that can only be learned in the wilderness.

Character. Covenant. Clarity. These were not given to us in the land of plenty. They were forged in the desert of not enough.

The wilderness taught us that delay is not denial—it is divine preparation. It showed us that it is entirely possible to walk with God and still not arrive on our timetable. It reminded us that victory may not be immediate, but obedience is always essential. And the longer we walked, the more we understood: the wilderness was not a curse. It was mercy in disguise.

If we had entered the promise too soon, we would have dragged Egypt in with us. We would have mistaken our comfort for our calling. We would have built new sanctuaries around old strongholds.

But the wilderness loosened our grip on the lies. It refined the vision until only what was holy remained. It matured our faith, not in the abundance of blessings, but in the barrenness of need. It taught us who we were—not when we had everything, but when we had nothing. It showed us that we could survive silence, walk through fire, and still believe.

So now, when we step into the promise, we do not enter blindly or naive. We step in with vision. We step in knowing how to lead with integrity, how to fight with purpose, how to wait with patience, and how to move forward with nothing but God's Word in our mouths and holy resolve in our bones.

We were not just delivered from something—we were delivered into something. Everything we need to steward this land was not born in comfort. It was born in the wild. It was forged in the fire of the wilderness.

The Promised Land was never merely about soil. It was never just about milk and honey, about borders and boundaries, about deeds and documents. It was never about who held the title to the land. It was always about who held the truth.

For us, inheritance is not defined by mansions or monuments. It is defined by breath—by the right to inhale without fear and exhale without apology. It is the right to speak without needing to translate our souls. It is the right to raise our children on land that does not consume their dreams but protects them.

We have been told that our inheritance was stolen. But we testify that it was never theirs to keep. What belongs to us cannot be held by empire, because it is secured in Heaven.

Our inheritance is not a hand-me-down passed from oppressors. It is a holy call to construct what they never had the vision—or the courage— to build. It is a world rooted in justice. It is a rhythm grounded in joy. It is a future that allows us to carry our history into peace, without needing to erase it.

The Promised Land is not just a physical location. It is a revelation. It is the moment we stopped waiting for permission to thrive. It is the space where we rewrite the script they handed us. It is the place where we redefine wealth—not as accumulation, but as collective flourishing. It is where legacy is measured not by what we possess, but by what we pass on. Not by what we own, but by what we release.

And this time—no snakes will slither through the grass wearing the disguise of lambs. There will be no hidden saboteurs pretending to serve the people while building private kingdoms. There will be no more betrayal in the backrooms. We will not relive the compromises of the 1960s and 1970s, when the dreams of the many were sold for the comfort of a few.

What belongs to all of us will not be seized by the greedy hands of the ambitious. It won't happen this time.

We do not inherit to hoard. We inherit to heal. We have come to build schools where only shacks once stood. We have come to plant trees where chains once hung. We have come to raise flags—not as symbols of conquest, but as declarations of covenant.

This time, we are not building the way they did. We are not here to extract. We are not here to dominate. We are not here to divide the land as if it were spoils of war. We are here to sanctify it. We see the land as sacred soil—soil that remembers every footprint of our ancestors and still finds a way to bloom.

This is the inheritance our people died dreaming about. And now, for the first time, that dream has a chance to live—not in mansions perched on hills, but in movements that make space. In communities that carry each other forward. In voices that no longer whisper but rise with holy fire.

We are the stewards now. We are the "reimaginers." We are the architects of what could be because we refused to let go of what should be. This is the Promised Land—not just returned, but reborn.

They told us the Promised Land was a reward. What they didn't tell us is how heavy it would be. Because every promise comes with a price. Every inheritance carries a burden. You don't step into freedom and automatically find rest. You step into the holy work of sustaining what was handed down through struggle and sacrifice.

This land—this sacred space of justice, dignity, and legacy—will not sustain itself. It requires our presence. It demands our protection. It calls for our cultivation. We must guard it—not with fear, but with faithfulness.

Now that we have arrived, we are the keepers. We are the keepers of the truth our ancestors whispered in cotton fields and scrawled into cell walls. We are the keepers of the songs they sang without instruments, only breath and hope. We are the keepers of a joy that refused to die, even when their bodies were broken.

We do not get to inherit and then disappear. We do not get to rest without bearing responsibility. This is sacred ground. And sacred ground must be stewarded with sacred care.

That means teaching what we were never taught. It means protecting what was once pillaged. It means building systems that bless rather than exploit. It means raising children who grow up believing they were born into a land that truly loves them back.

The Promised Land is not simply a place to live. It is a place to lead. And leadership will cost us far more than comfort ever did.

We do not desire to consume what we did not cultivate. We are called to be both planters and protectors. We must see the soil not merely as a symbol of achievement, but as a summons to serve.

Because the weight of the promise is not oppression—it is purpose. And if we fail to carry it with humility and intention, we risk turning our own inheritance into the very empire we once escaped.

So we remember—again and again. We remember every time we stand on land that our people were once forbidden to own. We remember every time we lift our voices in pulpits that our ancestors were never allowed to enter. We remember every time we vote, every time we build, every time we speak truth or choose to rest. We carry it all. We carry it with humility.

We carry it with power. We carry it with the deep understanding that the Promised Land does not belong to the loudest voice—it belongs to the most faithful hands.

Let no one be deceived: crossing into the promise does not mean the war has ended. It simply means that the battlefield has moved. Even in the Promised Land, we still face opposition.

The enemies are not always easy to identify. They do not always come dressed in uniforms. Sometimes they wear suits. Sometimes they hold microphones. Sometimes they disguise themselves inside policies, behind pulpits, or within the silence of those who should have spoken. Sometimes they look like fear pretending to be wisdom. Sometimes they wear the mask of tradition, but their roots are in pride. And sometimes, heartbreakingly, they look like us.

The real danger of arrival is believing that the fight is finished. But every step we take into promise threatens someone who profited from our bondage. Every wall we tear down reveals a foundation that someone else depended on. Every bridge we build disrupts the plans of gatekeepers. Every truth we tell rattles the very systems built to keep us quiet.

The Promised Land does not eliminate enemies—it exposes them. It shines a light on who never wanted us to be free. It reveals who benefitted from our delays. It uncovers who grew comfortable while we wandered in exile.

So yes, the land is blessed. But it is not empty. And not everyone will rejoice when we cross over.

The voices of resistance will rise. They will say: "They don't belong here. They didn't earn this. They are too loud, too radical, too Black, too Brown—too much." But here is what the wilderness taught us: we are not easily shaken anymore. We have fought without resources. We have prayed behind closed doors. We have bled in obscurity. We have led without titles, and with no map but obedience. And that is enough.

So when the enemies show up at the border, we do not run. We do not shrink. We build anyway. We build because the Promised Land is not only our reward—it is our responsibility.

We will not surrender this sacred ground to voices that never walked through the fire with us. We will not relinquish what we carried through wilderness to those who stood safely on the sidelines while we bore the weight of becoming.

Let the critics shout. Let the watchers stand still. We will raise our banners anyway. We will write new laws anyway. We will bless the land they never believed we would inherit. Because it was God who gave this land. It was the wilderness that prepared us. And now, no enemy at the gate can unseat what Heaven has already ordained.

Not everyone who marched made it in. And not everyone who made it in was ready to stay. Because the Promised Land is not just open territory—it is holy ground.

You do not enter it by coincidence. You do not dwell in it by entitlement. You walk in by covenant, with reverence in your stride and memory in your bones.

And so the question is not simply, "Did you survive the wilderness?" The deeper question is, "Did the wilderness transform you?" Because you cannot carry Egypt into Canaan. You cannot drag the mindset of slavery into the place of promise. You cannot colonize what God has declared sacred and still expect to receive the blessing.

Who, then, gets to enter? It will not be those who perform for applause. It will not be those who wear the mask of freedom but still trade in the currency of oppression. It will not be those who want the fruit but refuse the faithfulness required to cultivate it.

Only those who are ready to steward the soil are fit to inherit this land. Only those who can carry justice without vengeance in their hearts. Only those who remember that the promise was never meant for one—it was always meant for us all.

We do not inherit this land alone. We walk into it with memory guiding our steps, humility guarding our hearts, and our people carried on our backs. Our eyes are set on the horizon—not for what we can take, but for what we are called to build.

We walk into the Promised Land knowing it is not a stage for ego. It is a sanctuary for a new way of living. It is the place where the last are lifted—not exploited. It is where the wounded are welcomed, not discarded. It is where the very systems we dismantled in the wilderness are not allowed to return under a new name.

Some will cross just to conquer. Their only desire will be to dominate, not to deliver. They will come not to serve, but to rule. They will build altars—not unto God—but unto themselves, in a land that was always meant to glorify the One who brought us through.

They might make it through the gates. But they will not endure. Because God will never allow empire to reign in a place He has called promise.

This land was not given to those who seek to repeat the sins of the wilderness under new names and polished intentions. It was given to those who came out of exile carrying vision. It is for those who walked through fire and came out with reverence in their steps, with the flame still alive in their spirits, and with hands that remain open to Heaven.

Who gets to enter? It is those who understand that freedom is not a prize—it is a responsibility. It is those who know that liberation is not a finish line, but a way of life. It is those who will protect the promise with their lives, because they know the cost it took to stand where we now stand.

We did not arrive here by accident. We did not get here by favor alone. We walked through fire. We buried what could not come with us. We carried memory like a compass and covenant like armor.

Now we stand in the promise. And yes, the land flows with milk and honey. Yes, it is beautiful, abundant, and hard-won. Yes, it tastes like joy. Yes, it looks like healing.

But let us not be deceived by the abundance. This land does not exist without assignment. The milk was never meant for indulgence. The honey was never meant for hoarding. The promise was never only about receiving. It was always about becoming.

Now that we have entered, the real questions begin: What must we do with what we have inherited? Who will we feed with this abundance? What broken systems will we rebuild from the ground up? What lies will we dig out of the soil before we dare to plant something new?

Because every promise comes with a mandate. We are called to govern with righteousness. We are charged to build with integrity. We are summoned to love with power. We are commanded to protect the poor. And we are entrusted to pass on the fire without burning the next generation in the trauma we've survived.

This is not the end of the story. This is the beginning of legacy. This is the dawn of structure. This is the emergence of sacred order.

It is not just about what the land gives to us. It is about what we now return—back to our people, forward to our future, and upward to the God who carried us all the way here.

The wilderness taught us how to survive. But the promise will now teach us how to lead.

So, take your sandals off. The ground you are standing on is holy. But so is the charge to steward it well.

We did not simply arrive in a land flowing with milk and honey. It was the hands of our ancestors—their labor, their prayers, their blood—that made the land flow. It is not a miracle detached from history. It is the fruit of toil that was never compensated and seeds sown in sorrow.

The danger is not in the milk itself, nor in the wealth that comes from selling it. The danger is in forgetting why the milk flows in the first place. The threat is not in the sweetness of the honey or in the profits gained from it in the marketplace. The true threat lies in believing that sweetness signals the end of the struggle.

Because abundance is not always a blessing—especially when it is carried without understanding. Especially when it rests in hands untrained by history and unanchored by purpose.

The Promised Land is indeed full. It overflows with provision. It holds what we prayed for, what our ancestors dreamed of, and what the wilderness shaped us to receive. But we must heed the warning: if we forget the assignment, the abundance will consume us.

We will not be destroyed by famine—we will be destroyed by forgetfulness. We will not be undone by war—we will be undone by waste. When you have lived hungry long enough, the temptation is to gorge. The impulse is to hoard. The instinct is to guard what you never had, even at the expense of those around you.

But this land was not given to us so we could recreate Egypt with better branding. We were not delivered into freedom just to imitate the oppression we escaped. We were not rescued from scarcity to be ruled by greed. We were not set free to build palaces atop someone else's pain.

So the real question before us is not, "What will we eat?" The question now is, "What will we build?" Who will we feed with this abundance? And will we remember the wilderness—or will we let comfort erase the lessons that brought us here?

Because milk and honey are fragile things. They were never meant to be hoarded. They spoil when stored too long. They rot in selfish hands. They were meant to flow—to nourish, to circulate, and to bless.

God did not bring us into this land simply so we could rest. He brought us here so we could reign—with righteousness. We were placed here to govern the ground with reverence. We were called to make sure that no one else is left wandering while we feast inside a promise we did not earn alone.

Abundance without assignment is not just dangerous—it is deceptive. It seduces us into ease. It dulls our discernment. It tempts us to believe that arrival is the same as fulfillment.

But we have only just begun. Now that the land is in our hands, we must ask ourselves a sacred question: What will we do with it?

This land is not merely a promise—it is a mandate. It is not just a gift to enjoy; it is a charge to fulfill. Heaven is still watching to see what we will do with the milk, with the honey, and with the power that flows from both.

Milk and honey were never the end goal. They were never the destination. They were the evidence—proof that this land could sustain more than survival. They were signs that the season of mere existence was over, and the era of establishment had begun.

But let us not be fooled. With every flow of milk came the echo of commandments. With every taste of honey came the weight of divine mandates. We must remember this truth, because in the Kingdom of God, blessings never come detached. They are always tethered—to justice, to righteousness, and to memory.

God has never poured out abundance without also issuing instruction. He has never handed over land without calling His people into account. The promise was never about prosperity for its own sake. It was prosperity for the people—the elders, the widow, the orphan, and the stranger standing at the edge of the gate.

God said, "When you reap the harvest, leave some for the poor. When you rest, let the land rest too. And when you build, do not oppress."

The milk and the honey were not given for indulgence. They were given for distribution. They were not signs of status—they were signs of shared provision. They were never meant to be consumed by one, but to be extended to the many. They were signs that God had made a way—not for individuals to elevate themselves, but for a community to rise together.

Yet still we have distorted the meaning of the promise. We have preached a gospel of gain. We have built temples to celebrate our arrival, rather than altars to honor God's faithfulness. We have turned the promise into a pedestal, and status into the standard. But we are not here simply to receive. We are here to remember.

We must remember how long it took to get here. We must remember who didn't make it. We must remember that God did not bring us out of bondage just so we could recreate systems of oppression—this time in our own image.

This land must be governed by justice—not the kind that performs for attention, but the kind that prophesies with power. It must not exist for spectacle, but for sacred service. The justice we seek is not one that craves applause; it is one that pursues obedience. It does not bow to capitalism. It does not submit to colorism. It does not yield to the ease of convenience. It is the kind of justice that stands with the vulnerable and speaks truth even when that truth demands everything.

We are not merely recipients of a promise. We are reformers of a broken world. We are not called just to live in the land—we are called to transform it.

We are here to build cities of refuge, not monuments to ego. We are here to raise up righteous systems, not replicas of Pharaoh's throne in new clothing. Because it is not the land that makes us holy—it is how we steward the land that determines our holiness.

If we ignore that mandate—if we forget what we have been called to do—we risk forfeiting the very inheritance we were entrusted to steward. It will not be because God changed His mind. It will be because we stopped carrying His heart.

So let the milk flow. Let the honey sweeten our journey. But we must never forget this: the promise has always been tied to a mandate. The land was never meant to validate our arrival—it was always meant to reveal our obedience.

Crossing over is not the climax of the story. It is the beginning of a commissioning. The wilderness was our test. The Promised Land is our trust. It is a call to build. It is a summons to stewardship. And this calling is not just for us—it is for the generations that will rise from the soil beneath our feet because the real work begins after the victory.

It begins when the celebration ends. When the cameras leave. When the shouting fades and there are no more enemies in sight—just the holy, quiet question: "Now, what will you do with what you've been given?"

We did not come all this way simply to rest on blessings we did not build. We came to rebuild the world from the inside out. We came to repair what empire broke. To craft systems that look like Heaven. To plant equity in the very ground where injustice once reigned. To open doors where once there were only walls. To nourish bodies and souls in places where scarcity used to speak louder than hope.

This is Kingdom labor. And Kingdom labor does not begin with noise—it begins with order. It begins with structure. It starts with deep conversations around honest tables. The kickoff is with policies that protect. It advances with worship that overflows into action—into legislation, into land trusts, into health clinics and school boards, into clean water and unlocked doors.

A righteous people cannot live on promise alone. The promise must be built upon, or it will fade. We must become builders.

We do not just dwell here—we design here. We write policies infused with compassion. We raise up leaders who are shaped by justice. We plant gardens in food deserts. We place our hands on blueprints and declare with resolve: "This time, we will build it right."

This land will not be gentrified by greed. It will be governed by grace. It will be led by vision. It will be shaped by wisdom—wisdom forged in the fire of the wilderness. The true testimony is not that we entered the promise, but that we knew what to do with it once we got there.

We will not waste what was watered with the blood of our ancestors. We will not squander what was sanctified through suffering. And we will not sit in ease while others still wander in exile.

The work begins now. The Kingdom is in our hands. We will not stand still while others build. We are the architects. We are the caretakers. We are the righteous remnant. We rise with purpose. And we will keep building until the Promised Land becomes more than a dream—it becomes home.

Let us be clear: there is a difference between occupying the land and governing it. One builds fences to protect what belongs to them. The other lays foundations so that all may stand. One arrives and says, "Now that I'm here, I will guard what is mine." The other declares, "Now that I'm here, I will serve those who stand beside me."

Governance in the Kingdom of God is not rooted in domination—it flows from discipline. It does not defend territory with weapons, but with wisdom. It does not preserve power with walls, but with truth. It does not maintain control through force, but through covenant.

The Promised Land demands a different kind of leadership. It does not require Pharaoh's fist or Caesar's crown. It requires the posture of those who remember the cost of the journey. We cannot inherit this land and lead with the same hand that once crushed us. We cannot mimic the power structures we escaped and call that justice.

We must govern the promise with humility. We must lead with memory. We must understand that authority is not permission to dominate—it is a sacred trust that calls us into accountability.

This land was never meant for exploitation. It was meant for stewardship. It demands that we ask hard questions of ourselves: What kind of leaders will we become? What legacy will we leave behind? What culture will we cultivate now that we no longer serve Pharaoh, but walk in purpose?

The Promised Land remains fragile when held by those who forget. Any land that is misgoverned will, in time, become a new Egypt—cloaked in refined language, yet still bound by the same old chains.

When God gave the people the land, He also gave them laws—not to diminish their joy, but to preserve their justice. He gave them commandments not to restrict their abundance, but to protect their holiness. The laws were reminders that even milk and honey, without reverence, could become idols.

We must now govern with the same sacred commitment: with Sabbath woven into our rhythms, with righteousness embedded in our policies, with equity shaping our economy, and with mercy leading every decision we make. We are no longer the oppressed. We are the overseers now. And what we do with this power will echo through the generations that follow us.

Let it be remembered that when we entered the promise, we did not forget the pain that brought us here. We did not rule with pride. We did not hoard what Heaven handed to us. We governed with God in mind.

We can possess the land and still let it rot from within. We can inherit the promise and still allow weeds to choke the harvest if we do not protect the soil.

The soil is more than the earth beneath our feet. It is everything we cultivate. It is the culture we create, the ethics we uphold, the values we embody, and the vision we pursue. It is shaped by the atmosphere we tolerate, the systems we design, and the silences we allow to go unchecked.

The soil will remember what we plant, but it will also remember what we permit. If we fail to guard it, oppression will return—disguised in new language and dressed in modern clothes. Greed will mask itself as opportunity. Favoritism will present itself as wisdom. Old empire habits will find their way into these promised fields, camouflaged as progress.

Pharaoh is not always a man. Sometimes Pharaoh is a mindset. And if we are not vigilant, we will find ourselves acting like masters—free people who govern not from healing, but from wounds left unattended. That means we must unlearn old patterns and old ways of thinking.

That is why we must tend this soil like priests caring for the temple. We must walk the borders of our culture like prophets stationed on watchtowers. We must interrogate every new idea, every fresh initiative, every emerging system and ask with holy urgency: "Does this protect the people, or exploit them? Does this multiply equity, or simply rearrange who holds the power?"

The goal is not to flip the pyramid. The goal is to dismantle it. We must unlearn hierarchy. We must plant rest where rivalry once grew. We must sow truth where silence used to rule. We must dig up every lingering root of supremacy that survived the crossing.

We cannot afford to let trauma shape our laws. We cannot afford to let insecurity guard our gates. We cannot afford to build promised land empires while our neighbors still sleep outside the city walls.

We must guard this soil. We must keep it soft enough for joy, rich enough for justice, and clean enough for legacy to take root and flourish. What we allow in this moment will become what they inherit in the next.

This is sacred ground. And sacred ground must be watched with care, watered with intention, and protected with purpose. The land did not flow with milk and honey so we could build bigger barns. It flowed so everyone could get fed.

Abundance is not merely a blessing. It is a directive. God did not bring us into the promise so we could feast in isolation while others struggle to survive outside the gates. The Promised Land was never about having more. It has always been about sharing better.

Milk and honey are not symbols of wealth. They represent divine provision and nourishment. They speak of sustenance that satisfies, of resources that refresh the soul. These gifts were never meant to be hoarded. The promise remains incomplete until everyone is seated at the feasting table.

The promise is fulfilled when mothers no longer skip meals so their children can eat. It is realized when elders no longer ration medicine just to make it through the month. It is made real when our schools feed both minds and bodies, when the last are lifted and the line of the hungry grows shorter than the line for profit.

This is what the Kingdom of God's economics looks like. It is not built on charity or pity. It is rooted in justice and empowerment. In the Kingdom, food is access—not leverage. Resources are not determined by zip code or skin tone. The people are not meant to survive the promise. They are called to flourish within it.

We were not delivered from Egypt so we could build another empire with softer edges and a more palatable name. We are to disrupt the system. We are here to design a new world where the harvest is shared by all—not just those holding the tools.

Now we must ask ourselves the necessary questions. Are we creating spaces of hospitality, or are we constructing new hierarchies? Are we feeding egos, or are we feeding souls? Are we preserving our comfort while our communities still hunger for healing?

The Promised Land does not exist merely to satisfy our hunger. It exists to bring healing to the entire body—the body of our people, the body of our shared story, and the body of Christ.

So we stretch the table. We pour the milk. We share the honey. And we remember this one truth: the clearest proof of our promise is that no one leaves the table hungry.

We have entered the land. We have crossed through the wilderness, confronted the borders, torn down the walls, and built the bridges. We have stepped into the promise with calloused hands and sanctified vision.

And in this place of abundance, we have learned that milk and honey come with mandates. Abundance is not the final reward. It is the beginning of responsibility. The Promised Land is not a resting place. It is a rebuilding place.

As we plant, as we govern, and as we guard, we must turn our attention to one institution that cannot afford to stay silent. One body that cannot remain on the sidelines of this movement. That body is the Church.

By Church, we do not mean only the buildings with steeples or the gatherings in pews. We are speaking of the collective body of those who claim the name of Christ. If the Church was meant to be a beacon, then it must burn with something more than candles and programs. It must burn with righteous fire.

It must burn with memory. It must burn with repentance. It must burn with justice that flows like a river—not justice that drips like a slow trickle on Sunday mornings.

The Church must give account for the ways it has blessed the empire while crucifying the prophets. It must reckon with the times it hoarded milk and honey while the hungry waited outside its doors. It must confess the ways it spiritualized oppression and silenced truth in the name of order.

And so, we extend the invitation. This is not a subpoena to the stage. It is not an occasion for the spotlight. It is a call to the work, a visit with the Divine.

It is a call to the altar of accountability. An invitation to the table of redistribution. A sacred summons to truth-telling and reconciliation that costs something—because real redemption always does.

This is an invitation to the Church. This call is not casual; it demands a response drenched in godly sorrow. The Church is summoned to join the builders. It is commissioned to repent with power, to lead with unwavering integrity, and to speak with holy fire. It is charged to carry the weight of the promise alongside those who bled and sacrificed to see it fulfilled.

The Promised Land remains incomplete until the Church stops performing and begins prophesying. It will not be whole until the Church abandons the protection of comfort and partners fully with the Kingdom—so that heaven is not only hoped for but seen on earth.

The time for silence has ended. The invitation has been extended. The mandate stands before us, unmistakable. Church—will you answer?

12

AN INVITATION TO THE CHURCH

"Stand at the crossroads and look; ask for the ancient paths, ask where the good way is, and walk in it, and you will find rest for your souls."

JEREMIAH 6:16, NIV

Heaven is no longer whispering. It is shouting. And still, we scroll. Still, we stall. Still, we stuff our ears with noise, pretending we can't hear the alarm sounding across the soul of the Church. But God is not confused. And He is not quiet. The Spirit has spoken—and this time, the shutdown is divine.

None of this is theory. It is not conceptual or abstract. It is real. I lived it.

On a cold December night in 2016, God gave me a picture—not just for me, but for His Church. At the time, I was still working as a real estate broker and with a commercial real estate data analytics firm. My days were spent fielding numbers and negotiations. That week, I had also been walking hospital hallways, visiting my mother-in-law. When I came home, I was exhausted—depleted in body, mind, and spirit. I didn't want a word from heaven. I wanted a distraction. I wanted to zone out with a movie and let sleep take me.

That was the plan. But heaven had a different agenda.

I scrolled through channels. I flipped to Netflix. I wanted something to soothe me, to entertain me, to numb me. And in the midst of that motion, I heard the Spirit of God speak clearly: *"Turn off the TV."*

I didn't obey. I kept scrolling.

Moments later, the TV shut down. I assumed it was just a glitch—nothing spiritual. Just technology doing what technology does. But when I turned the TV back on, restarted the app and reentered my login—something that had never been required before—I heard the Spirit again. This time, the voice was more urgent: *"Turn off the TV."*

Still, I resisted. Still, I searched. Still, I chose comfort over command.

Again, the TV and platform shut down. Again, I was forced to re-enter everything.

This time, I paused. And I obeyed.

I turned off the TV. And the moment I did, the atmosphere shifted. A divine weight settled into the room like smoke from a burning altar. Heaven had entered—and this time, it came not with entertainment, but with an encounter. Not just for me, but for the Church. This is where we are.

This is the condition of the modern Church. God is still speaking—but we are still scrolling. We are still distracted, still disobedient, still prioritizing convenience over consecration. And just like He did with me, the Spirit has shut the system down. This time, we will not be able to log in the same way. We will need a new password. A new posture. A holy fear.

Christ is calling the Church to attention. But we keep flipping. Flipping through our spiritual entertainment options. Consuming sermons like snack food. Customizing conviction. Bypassing the cross for content that fits neatly within our comfort zones.

The Church is not silent because God has gone silent. We are silent because we have reduced Him to background noise. We have shoved Jesus into a spiritual closet, calling on Him only in moments of desperation.

We treat the Holy Spirit like a genie, a performer, a prop to dress up our Sunday services.

The show is over. What we are hearing now is not the silence of an absent God—it is the silence that follows our disobedience. Heaven has already spoken. A warning has gone out. The system is crashing. The stage we built on spectacle is crumbling. And the endless scrolling through distraction must come to an end.

God is not here to entertain us. He is not performing for our approval. He is speaking with urgency. He is warning with love. And He is waiting—patiently, but not passively—for His people to return to obedience.

We are standing at a pivotal moment. We are positioned on sacred ground, but our ears are overwhelmed with noise and our hands are preoccupied with distractions. What He is saying to the Church now is the same thing He said to me that night: "Turn it off."

Turn off the noise that drowns out conviction. Turn off the self-worship masked as spirituality. Turn off the performative praise and lights-only revival. Turn off the counterfeit call that values platforms more than it values His presence. And His presence is felt because the one leading has been in His presence and it's not only based on gifts alone.

He still has something to say but we have rejected the sacrifice and reached for sensation. We have turned away from the Spirit and chosen spectacle instead. We have abandoned the cross and lusted after the crown. But Christ never said, "Take the crown." He said, "Take up your cross." And taking up the cross means dying.

Die to ego. Die to empire. Die to domination dressed up as doctrine. Die to the desire to use His name as a brand to build personal kingdoms.

So what must die? We must die—not just our flesh, but our will. Our hunger for applause must be put in a coffin and buried. Our need to be right while others suffer wrong has to die. Our comfort that comes at the expense of our neighbor's cry must come to an end.

The Church has a mandate. Christ has already fulfilled His part. When He said, "It is finished," He meant that the rest would be accomplished through us.

Will we respond to the call of Heaven? Or will we continue to cry out for God to move while we remain unmoved—seated in silence, paralyzed by comfort, and unwilling to act on the very prayers we pray?

We are not spectators. We are the Ecclesia—the called-out ones. We are citizens of heaven and ambassadors of a Kingdom not built by human hands. That identity makes us more than theological—we are political in the purest sense of the word. Our faith is not just found in Scripture; it must be found alive in our lives. That is how God moves mountains.

Our assignment is not limited to the sanctuary. It is not fulfilled simply by Sunday gatherings. Our assignment is to represent the justice of God in a land that thrives on injustice. It is to proclaim liberty to those in captivity. It is to break generational yokes. It is to love our neighbors—not in word only, but through wounds we are willing to tend, even when we did not cause them.

This is not only a call to repentance. This is a call to restitution.

We must repent for the Church's long-standing complicity in the systems of racism, colonialism, white supremacy, and greed. We must pay for what we inherited—the broken altars and false teachings passed down from forefathers who preached bondage and dared to call it blessing.

We must mourn the atrocities done in the name of Christ that looked nothing like Christ. When Jesus was confronted by the Pharisees and Sadducees, He named the greatest commandments without ambiguity: Love God. Love your neighbor.

So the question remains: Who is your neighbor? And how are you loving them when their history has been erased, their identity denied, and their blood sewn into your flag but not welcomed in your sanctuary? Are they only welcome to sit in the pews, or are they trusted to help govern the body they belong to?

The blood of the descendants of slaves flows through this nation. It flows through your veins. It is interwoven. It is undeniable. And it will either rise as the leaven that lifts us all into a new way of being—or it will remain a stain that marks our generation as the one who knew the truth and still refused to change.

Water is flowing from the rock again. But it will only be poured out for those who strike it in obedience. We sing, "Lift every voice and sing,"[6] but when every voice is lifted in pain—do we really listen?

We are the Church. We are the light of the world. A city set on a hill cannot be hidden. So why have we gone quiet?

We keep waiting for another Azusa Street revival. What if the delay is our fault? What if God is waiting for our repentance first?

The wind is blowing again—strong, holy, and unrelenting. It crashes like the waves I once watched in Cancun, where the sea struck the shoreline over and over with divine pressure, reshaping the land beneath it. In the same way, the Spirit is pressing against the borders of our comfort. He is calling. Loud. Clear. Relentless.

But will we scroll past Him again? Or will we finally turn off the noise—so we can turn toward His voice?

Because if we don't, the pulpits will grow colder still. And when pulpits fall silent, the streets begin to speak—not with tongues of fire, but with sirens, with protests, and with public grief. When the Church stops prophesying, the culture starts screaming.

We are standing at a sacred crossroads. And now, we must ask ourselves: What kind of Church will we become?

Will we reclaim our prophetic voice, or protect our public image? Will we carry the cross, or polish our brand? Will we love with action, or retreat into lifeless doctrine?

---

6. (Johnson, 1900)

The invitation has already been issued. The time is now. And this—this is what happens when pulpits go silent.

There was a time when pulpits thundered with righteousness. Prophets once stood tall—not to prophesy about cars, cash, and comfort, but to cry out for justice in the streets. Sanctuaries were once shelters for the suffering, not platforms for the celebrated.

But something has shifted. The fire that once forced Pharaoh to bow now flickers beneath fog machines. The Word that once loosed the chains of the enslaved is now whispered in buildings too afraid to say, "Black Lives Matter." The cross that once marked a revolution has been reduced to a logo—clean, marketable, and void of conviction.

The pulpits went silent. This silence did not come because God ceased to speak. It came because the Church refused to listen.

We once heard the thunder of truth. Now we echo the sound of self. We no longer wait for heaven's whisper. Instead, we manufacture messages, stamp them with God's name, and sell them like merchandise. What we call revelation is often greed in disguise. What we call presence is too often performance.

And though many still invoke the Spirit, it's more about performing from the gifts God gave—not because God had imparted new revelation. What they truly seek is the spotlight.

They call it ministry—but it is marketing. They claim it is divine—but it is scripted. The tragedy is not that God has ceased to speak. The tragedy is that we have grown content mistaking noise for anointing, applause for approval, and profit for purpose.

Comfort has become our king. Profit has become our pursuit. Pleasing the masses has taken precedence over pleasing Heaven. And now, the Church no longer recognizes the voice of its own Shepherd.

We traded conviction for compatibility. We stopped telling the truth when it threatened the offering plate. We stopped preaching repentance if it risked offending political alliances. We no longer disrupted the systems of Pharaoh; instead, we took a seat at his table. And the silence was deafening.

It was deafening when enslaved bodies were whipped beneath the shadow of the cross. It was deafening when pastors blessed the burning of crosses on front lawns. It was deafening when churches locked their doors during civil rights marches but flung them open for potlucks and revivals.

The silence is still deafening now. It roars when pulpits refuse to speak about racial injustice. It echoes when pastors preach peace while ignoring the war outside their sanctuaries. It screams when churches claim neutrality, even when Jesus Himself never did.

Silence is not neutrality. Silence is complicity. Every time the pulpit stays quiet, another soul walks out believing God is indifferent to their pain. Another child grows up assuming faith and justice are strangers. Another movement rises from the streets because the Church refused to rise in the Spirit. Let us make no mistake: this silence is not sacred—it is sinful.

We are not called to quiet compliance. We are called to be witnesses. Witnesses tell the truth, even when it costs them. Witnesses speak up, even when it shakes the room. Witnesses preach Christ crucified and communities set free.

If the Church is silent in the face of injustice, it is no longer the Body of Christ. It becomes the ghost of empire—cloaked in Christ's name but void of His Spirit.

But there is still time. Time to repent. Time to return. Time to raise our voices again—not for applause, not for platform, but because the One who called us is still calling.

We are no longer wandering in the wilderness. We are standing still, not because the Spirit has stopped moving, but because the Church has stopped following.

We are at a crossroads. One path is wide and well-worn. It leads to packed pews, polished sermons, and predictable worship. It is safe. It is celebrated. But it is powerless—because it demands nothing of us and changes nothing around us.

The other path is narrow and costly. It does not offer applause—only alignment. It calls for the tearing down of idols—not just golden calves, but the gods of comfort, nationalism, whiteness, and control. It calls for a Church that is willing to lose relevance in order to gain righteousness.

The Church cannot stand at this crossroads forever. There is no neutral ground—no third option. There's only complicity or covenant.

Will we preserve our image? Or will we embody Christ? Because the world is not confused about who Jesus is. They are confused about who we are, and they have every right to be.

We have worn the cross on our chests, just as Superman wears the "S" on his, while refusing to carry it on our backs. We have baptized power and mistaken it for anointing. We have cloaked silence in spiritual language and called it discernment. We have hoarded platforms and convinced ourselves it was purpose. But God is not confused. He knows exactly who His Church is supposed to be. He is waiting to see if we still desire Him more than we desire to be liked. More than we desire to be right. More than we desire to remain comfortable.

This is the line in the sand. Will we continue to protect our buildings, our budgets, and our brands? Or will we burn our idols to the ground and rise with holy fire? Because the next move of God will not fit inside the structures we have built. It will not be confined to stained glass windows or steeples. It will not wait for a stage or a microphone. It is already moving—among the misfits, the mourners, and the marginalized. It is breaking out among those pushed out of the sanctuary but still attuned to the voice of the Shepherd in the street.

The Church stands at a crossroads. Heaven is watching to see whether we will bow to the comfort of the familiar or rise to the call of the Kingdom.

Heaven is waiting for us to understand that the Church is the Kingdom—that they do not operate separately.

Repentance is not a trend. It is not a press release. It is not a carefully worded social media post crafted in the safety of a boardroom. Repentance is rupture. It is the holy tearing of garments that never belonged to the Kingdom in the first place. It is the public confession of private complicity. It is the cleansing of a Church that has grown far too comfortable with its own corruption.

Yes, the Church must repent. We must repent not only for what we have said, but for what we failed to say. For what we silenced. For what we funded. For what we platformed and protected.

We must repent for preaching obedience while ignoring oppression. We must repent for clinging to nationalism while abandoning the Gospel. For wrapping the Bible in a flag and calling it the truth. For preaching personal holiness while refusing to confront systemic sin.

We must repent for our obsession with buildings and branding while souls bleed just outside our sanctuary doors. We must repent for turning the mission of Christ into a marketing strategy. For choosing donors over disciples. For keeping our churches white—not because of theology, but because of culture and comfort.

We must repent for the theologies that justified slavery, segregation, colonization, and silence. We must repent for weaponizing Scripture against the poor, the Black, the Brown, the immigrant, the queer, the woman, and the wounded. We must repent for lifting our hands in worship while pressing our feet against the necks of the oppressed.

We must repent for calling trauma rebellion, and for calling justice division. We must repent for baptizing politicians while crucifying prophets. We must repent for demanding civility while ignoring suffering. We must repent for loving order more than we loved people.

It is not enough to repent behind closed doors. When sin has been

public, repentance must be public as well. The words alone are not suffi-
cient. We must bring restitution. We must initiate repair. We must change
direction. We must release what we once clung to for power.

The Church does not need another conference. It needs a funeral. It
requires a funeral for every idol we built in God's name. It needs a funeral
for every power structure we embraced and mistook for His presence. It
needs a funeral for every lie we dressed in theology and dared to call truth.

This moment is not about guilt. It is about getting clean. Revival will
not come to a Church still entangled with Pharaoh. We say we want a
move of God but God will not dwell in a house built on injustice.

So, the question is not whether God is still speaking. The question is
whether we are finally ready to hear Him. And if we are, then let repentance begin.

We have wept. We have confessed. We have repented. Now it is time to
rise. But we cannot rise into what we once were. We must rise into what
we were always meant to become.

Resurrection is not about returning. It is about transformation. A Church
that dies to itself cannot return to performance. It must return in power.

This is not the time to rebuild what God has already torn down. This is
not the time to rebrand what must be reborn. This is the time to rise. We
must rise into prophetic leadership that disrupts the status quo. Leadership that does not serve platforms but washes feet. Leadership that speaks
the truth, even when the truth is costly. Leadership that leads from humility and kneels in prayer before it ever stands in authority. Leadership that
stands beside the bruised, the broken, and the bound—not out of pity,
but because of covenant.

We must rise into righteous redistribution—of land, of wealth, of power,
and of platform. The Church in Acts did not hoard its abundance. The
people laid what they had at one another's feet so that no one went without. No one was hungry. No one was forgotten.

We must rise in that same Spirit. A Spirit where justice is not just a theory but becomes a tangible table where all are welcome. A place where our budgets preach louder than our bulletins.

We must rise into radical inclusion. We are not called to offer mere tolerance. We are not called to parade tokenism and pretend it is justice. We are called to extend a sacred and intentional invitation into the full body of Christ. This body makes room for those who were once rejected. It restores their dignity. It honors their presence. It makes them visible— not as exceptions, but as essential.

This is the call of the Spirit. The Spirit is calling us to cast out every remnant of the colonial mindset that has distorted the Gospel. He is asking us to lay down our obsession with being the moral majority, especially when we lack the moral authority to lead. The Spirit is urging us to break our allegiance with empire and every system that exalts power over people. He is commanding us to proclaim Christ crucified—not for performance, but for the liberation of communities that have long been bound. He is calling us to set the captives free.

We must become the Church that Jesus recognizes. We must become a Church that carries His Spirit with integrity, not just His name in vanity. We must live the Sermon on the Mount, not merely recite it. We must walk among the wounded with compassion and conviction, refusing to exchange our anointing for applause or popularity.

The world is not desperate for a louder Church filled with noise. It is crying out for a lower Church—one that kneels to wash feet in humility. A Church that stoops to serve without demanding recognition. A Church that lifts others from the ashes without needing to elevate itself in the process.

This is our moment to rise. How we rise will determine whether the next generation finds refuge in the Church or runs from it.

We were never meant to be the gatekeepers of grace. But somewhere along the way, we confused stewardship with control. We began to believe that we were the ones who could decide who belongs, as though Heaven's guest list needed our approval.

But the Kingdom of God is not locked behind our gates. It is already in motion. The Spirit of God is not waiting for our permission. He is already moving—through the streets, inside prison cells, in the poetry of the marginalized, in the songs of the forgotten, and in the groans of those we labeled as too radical or too real.

The Church was never meant to be a fortress. It was always meant to be a fountain. We were never called to be bouncers at the door. We were called to be builders at the table.

God is not asking us to manage revival. He is calling us to join it. He is inviting us to partner with what He is already birthing in the earth. He is summoning us to walk beside those who were building altars in hidden places long before we paid attention. We must open our eyes to the truth: some of the loudest and most powerful moves of God are unfolding without a single choir robe, without a pulpit, and without a sermon outline. They are happening where hunger is deep, where humility is present, and where control has been surrendered.

Now is the time to dismantle our elitism. We must lay down the pulpit-polishing, platform-chasing mindset that insists God only moves through our titles and our timelines.

If we are honest, God has been moving all along. He has been moving through the very ones we overlooked. He has spoken through the exiled prophets we dismissed. He has preached through the single mothers who carry fire in their bellies and faith in their bones. He has stirred justice through the community organizers who lead with sacred rage and holy vision. He has declared truth through the youth who prophesy not just with their words but with the very witness of their lives. He has revealed glory through the artists who dare to dream out loud what pulpits have been too afraid to say.

This is not a threat to the Church. This is an invitation to become the Church once more. We are not called to be gatekeepers, standing guard over who gets in. We are called to be co-laborers—partners in the work of redemption, restoration, and justice.

We must stop guarding the gates of a Kingdom we did not build, do not own, and cannot contain. Revival will not follow our order of service. It will look like Jesus flipping tables. It will look like the Spirit descending on people with no titles. It will look like righteousness flowing outside our walls faster than our leadership teams can convene.

And when we finally release our grip on control, we will find the Spirit already waiting for us—hands extended, voice steady, whispering the words He has always said: "Come. Work with Me."

This is the altar call. It does not summon us to the front of a sanctuary, but to the very edge of history. It is a Spirit-breathed, open-handed appeal to a Church that still has time to turn, to awaken, and to return to its first love.

It is not too late. That is the mercy of it all. After the silence, after the compromise, after the forgetting and the failure—the invitation still stands. God is still speaking. He is still calling. He is still sending wind and wave to wake us up—not to shame us, but to restore us.

He has not shut the door. He has not revoked the mandate. He has not changed His mind about the Church, but He is changing His method.

God is raising up voices outside the camp. He is anointing those we ignored and overlooked. He is reviving hearts that have never stepped foot inside a sanctuary. He is pouring out His Spirit on all flesh—not just on those with titles or credentials.

And still, He invites us. He compels us to participate—to repent, to rebuild, to release our grip on control and reclaim the courage we lost. He is calling us to become the Church that Heaven designed, not the version history distorted.

This invitation is not about perfection. It is about posture. Are we open? Are we listening? Are we willing to lose what we built, so we can become what He desires?

The invitation does not come with fanfare. It comes like a whisper. It motions us like a breeze asking us to turn. It is like a wave crashing against the rigid shoreline of our traditions.

If we miss it, we will find ourselves clinging to what was, while the Spirit moves forward without us. But if we respond—if we lay down our pride, our politics, and our performances—we will be swept into something holy, something so alive, something beautiful, wild, untamable, and redemptive. Revival is not reserved. It is revealed and it is revealed to those who are ready.

Here is the invitation: to the pastors and the prophets, the pew-sitters and the prodigals. To the elders and the skeptics. To those who stayed, and those who walked away: Come back. Come low. Come ready.

The invitation is still open. And Jesus is still waiting for a Church that looks like Him.

13

DECLARATION OF DEMAND FOR REPARATIONS

"This is what the LORD Almighty, the God of Israel, says to all those I carried into exile from Jerusalem to Babylon: 'Build houses and settle down; plant gardens and eat what they produce.'"

JEREMIAH 29:4-5 NIV

T his is not a request. This is not a plea. This is a declaration. A holy indictment. We are not asking for charity. We are demanding justice. We are not begging for favor. We are insisting on repair.

The time for silence has ended. The season of evasion and delay is over. What now stands before us is the call for restitution. A divine and generational reckoning has come not just from us—but from God. It is a summons to the United States and to every government, institution, corporation, and private citizen who has profited from this nation's original sin—*slavery*—to come to account.

This is not a polite request. This is not a whispered plea. This is a demand echoing from the blood-soaked soil and the bones buried beneath it. A demand born from centuries of unpaid labor, unreconciled grief, and unacknowledged injustice.

The trumpet has sounded. The books are being opened. And every ledger stained with stolen time, stolen bodies, and stolen wealth must now be balanced.

We are grieving what we do not know. We are mourning a place we have never touched—yet somehow, we still call it home. The lyrics echo from a song written by Charlie Smalls and performed by Stephanie Mills in the Broadway musical *The Wiz*: "When I think of home, I think of a place where there's love overflowing." But for us—descendants of the enslaved—that is a melody we've never truly lived.

For the descendants of the transatlantic slave trade, "home" has not been a refuge. It has been a battleground. It has been a landfill layered with the bones of our ancestors and of broken promises. It has been a cesspool of mob lynchings, police brutality, and the recycled stench of systemic discrimination.

It is not because of who we are, but because of the skin we wear. This land has been polluted with the odor of racism, robbery, and bloodshed. And still, we are told to be quiet. Still, we are handed policies like pacifiers, shoved into our mouths to silence our righteous cries.

But we are not infants. We are heirs. And we will no longer be pacified.

We will not accept the excuses of a generation that washes its hands like Pilate, claiming innocence while living on the interest of stolen labor. "We didn't do it," they say—yet they live inside systems their ancestors built and from which they still benefit. So, we say this plainly: silence is participation. Inaction is complicity. And deflection is no longer acceptable.

We are not asking to be soothed. We are demanding to be served. We are not crying to be coddled—we are crying because we are hungry. We are hungry for the justice that nourishes a people into perpetuity. We are hungry for the restitution that feeds not just one generation, but every generation to come. And the time to feed us is now.

We grieve the family we never knew. We mourn the milestones we missed. We shed tears over the surnames we were forced to forget. We lament the lineages erased. We weep for the memories vanished. Our very identities were rewritten—first in chains, then in laws, then in textbooks that told lies about who we were. Families were split apart not once, but twice—first by the slave ships, then again by American soil. Marriages were dismissed. Children were sold. Love was outlawed. And still, the grief lingers—unspoken, but ever-present. It has simmered for centuries and now rises as a righteous rage that no longer fits inside Sunday sermons or campaign slogans.

Yet even with all of that, we were not scattered by accident. We were planted with purpose. We were planted to break open hardened ground with our cries and our songs. We were planted to prove that even in a field soaked in blood, life still pushes through. We were planted to carry memory in our bones and justice in our breath. We were sown as witnesses and as weapons—not to destroy with bitterness, but to dismantle with holy fire.

We were sown to remember—to rise, to rebuild what was ruined, to redeem what was rejected, and to awaken what was buried beneath centuries of ash and erasure. We were sown to confront empires built on backs and banks, and to declare, with authority: no more.

We were sown to plant vineyards in graveyards. We have been strategically placed to birth hope where horror once reigned. We were planted to become both seed and sword—breaking, building, and blessing with every step. We were positioned to carve rivers through deserts, to reclaim cities as sanctuaries, and to rebuild the ancient ruins with hands that never forgot how to praise through pain.

We were not scattered. We were sent to this soil. We were planted here for this moment. We were sent with heaven's strategy to confront the evils of empire.

And now, the time of harvest is here. We rise, not just to remember but to act. And rising means more than poetry. It is more than tears. It means policies. It means payments. It means property. It means power.

We will not enter this next season carrying old wounds and still expecting new fruit. We cast off shame. We renounce the bitterness that tries to rot the roots. We hold our hands open for justice—not charity. We hold open our hands for covenant—not compromise. And yes, we hold our hands open for reparations—not pacification.

Wherever we have been scattered—America, the Caribbean, South America, Europe—our presence is not a mistake. It is proof—that we survived, that we are unstoppable, and that we are the ones who bear the image of ancestors too strong to die.

And now, we build. We assemble even in stormy seasons—when the winds of white supremacy blow fierce and the air tastes of empire. In that very moment, God whispers: "Stay. Settle. Build. Plant the seeds of your future in the very soil of your struggle. Let your roots go deep, because transformation happens here."

So here is our appeal. This is not a request for charity. This is a prophetic demand for restitution that comes from God Almighty. A Declaration of Demand for Reparations—to the United States government, to the corporations that profited, to the churches that prayed over bondage, and to the private citizens who still benefit from the theft.

We will no longer wait. We will no longer be pacified. And we will not stop until justice is not only spoken—but served.

A DEMAND FOR REPARATIONS

We, the descendants of the enslaved of the traumatic and inhumane system setup through the Transatlantic Slave Trade, demand the following from the federal government of the United States of America:

1. We demand a formal and national acknowledgment of slavery as a crime against humanity, accompanied by a public apology.

2. We demand Congress to amend the Voting Rights Act of 1965[7], granting not just voting rights into perpetuity but also granting civil liberties—not just civil rights—to all without consideration of race, color, or previous condition of servitude, as it was previously written. Congress will end the 25-year reassessment mandate of voting rights once and for all. This amendment to the Act will also reinstate the voting rights of felons who pay restitution for their crimes.

3. We demand payment of $170,169 per descendant of the transatlantic slave trade's enslaved persons to be set up in an established Trust (Sovereign Wealth Fund) that will be managed by us, for us. (See Appendix for details of how this total was derived.)

4. We demand Congress to establish a Freedom Sovereign Wealth Fund (FSWF) to be funded by governments, businesses/corporations, institutions, churches, and any private citizen who wants to align with our mission. This fund will be managed by us, for us, without governmental interference or oversight through its Commission.

---

7. Congress. (n.d.-b). *Voting rights act (1965)*. National Archives and Records Administration. https://www.archives.gov/milestone-documents/voting-rights-act

5. We will establish from among our own communities an FSWF Commission to fund long-term, community development and outreach in predominantly Black and descendant-of-slavery communities.

6. We demand that the United States government offer through the GSEs or HUD land grants, zero-interest home loans, and tax-exempt business grants to Black descendants of American slavery.

7. We demand Congress fund HBCUs and educational institutions serving Black communities with reparative, not performative, generosity.

8. We demand all student loan debt for descendants of slaves to be cancelled as a form of educational restitution without a taxable event.

9. We demand that from this point forward; no descendant of slaves will ever pay for education. Our education will be funded by an additional 3 percent national sales tax that will be collected by the Treasury Department with regular reporting to the FSWF.

10. We demand that Congress enact legislation requiring all state and local governments rewrite American history to include accurate details of the United States' involvement in the Transatlantic Slave Trade and include all traumatic events in black history accounts since and including current details.

11. We demand state and local Boards of Education, with legislation enacted by Congress to teach all of American history, including the positive contributions of the enslaved and their descendants in the establishment and continued greatness of this nation—not just during Black History month, but all year, every year.

These lessons must go beyond just Martin Luther King, Jr and Harriett Tubman.

12. We demand that all historical books and publications written for schools and institutions of higher learning be republished to accurately depict the details of slavery and the history of the descendants of slaves through modern times.

13. We demand that all State and local governments must require all police departments to establish cultural sensitivity training and community service as part of new-hire processes and ongoing missions for veteran officers. Additionally, they must avoid overreach in carrying out their duties and only address imminent and probable threats. They must also implement stricter hiring processes (background checks, including social media account reviews, that would uncover any known histories of radical association affiliations, etc.) to ensure that those who want to harm people of color are not hired.

To Corporations that Profited from Slavery:

1. We demand public admission and documentation of how profits were built on slave labor.

2. We demand the creation of multi-billion-dollar restoration funds to be contributed to the FSWF that will be designated for economic development in affected Black communities. Any business, corporation, institution or other entity that contributes to the FSWF will be granted a 2-for-1 dollar tax write off mandated by Congress.

3. We demand redirection of 10% of annual profits into the FSWF to ensure effective implementation of generational wealth-building

initiatives including homeownership, health care access that includes mental health, and employment training.

4. We demand an establishment of scholarships specifically for descendants of American chattel slavery.

To Religious Institutions and Denominations:

1. We demand a confession for the role played in justifying and enabling slavery, segregation, and white supremacy.

2. We demand a return of land and resources acquired during slavery and Jim Crow eras to Black communities.

3. We demand that you fund mental health and trauma-healing centers in cities ravaged by racial violence and church-sanctioned silence.

4. We demand you commit to reparative justice in theology, curriculum, and leadership structures.

To Private Citizens and Allies:

1. We demand you pay forward land, inheritance, and privilege through reparative giving, asset sharing, and advocacy into the FSWF.

2. We demand you support Black-owned businesses not with charity, but with covenant. (See Appendix for explanation)

3. We demand a push for legislation that dismantles systems of economic apartheid.

4. We demand you create pathways for mutual accountability and truth-telling in your spheres of influence.

ACTIONABLE DEMANDS FOR HOUSING JUSTICE AND REPARATIVE EQUITY

1. Restitution through Land and Property Ownership

- We demand transfer of publicly held or tax-foreclosed properties to long-standing residents and descendants of enslaved peoples at no cost or highly subsidized rates, giving us preference over other interested parties. Priority must be for first-time homeowners.

- We demand the establishment of land trusts controlled by the FSWF and distributed for the use and benefit of descendants of slaves, not corporations or outside developers.

2. Reparative Housing Grants

- We demand federally funded grants be established for Black homebuyers descended from slavery, with no repayment obligation, to correct centuries of exclusion from housing markets.

- We demand retroactive mortgage relief for families impacted by redlining, predatory lending, and urban renewal displacement.

3. Reform of Zoning and Housing Codes

- We demand an overhaul of zoning laws that reinforce racial segregation and displacement.

- We demand that any developer seeking to construct or significantly alter property in historically Black neighborhoods be required to form a Joint Venture with a Black-owned business and prioritize hiring Black residents from that community to lead and labor in the revitalization efforts.

- We demand an elimination of discriminatory barriers that prevent multi-generational living, co-ownership, and alternative housing models that serve Black communities.

4. Guaranteed Right of Return

- We demand first-right opportunities for displaced families to return to gentrified neighborhoods at original cost-adjusted prices.

- We demand legal protections to prevent mass evictions tied to redevelopment schemes and public-private partnerships.

5. Community Control Over Development

- We demand the establishment of Black-led community review boards with binding authority over new housing developments in historically marginalized neighborhoods.

- We demand that a majority of public housing and redevelopment funds go to local Black-owned construction firms, architects, and planners.

6. Truth and Reconciliation in Housing Policy

- We demand a national acknowledgment of past and present housing discrimination via a federal Housing Justice Commission.

- We demand public education campaigns documenting the history of redlining, urban renewal, and land theft against Black communities.

7. Long-Term Equity Investment

- We demand the creation of a Federal Reparations Housing Trust funded by *banks, corporations, and insurance companies* that profited from slavery, Jim Crow laws, and discriminatory lending and administered through the FSWF.

- We demand that any individual who contributes to the FSWF receive dollar for dollar tax write offs mandated by Congress and enforced by the IRS. Any business, corporation, institution or other entity that contributes to the FSWF must be granted a 2-for-1 dollar tax write off mandated by Congress.

- We demand annual disbursements to support intergenerational wealth-building through homeownership, entrepreneurship, education, and community infrastructure.

These are not dreams. These are demands. They are not optional. They are overdue. They are the rightful summons for what has been stolen, ignored, buried, and denied. These are the responsibilities of a government that built its wealth on bondage. These are the bills long past due. Until these demands are met with urgency and integrity, the cry for justice will not be silent. Neither will God.

This is not just about repairing homes. This is about repairing the soul of a nation.

WE DECLARE: WE WILL NOT BE MOVED.

We declare that the days of stolen land, stolen labor, and stolen legacy are coming to an end. We are not beggars at the gate. We are the builders of the house. Our blood is in the bricks. Our stories are in the soil. And our dignity will not be bulldozed to make way for anyone's profit.

To every policy that sought to erase us—we respond with undeniable presence. To every project that displaced us—we return with divine purpose. To every system that profited from our pain—we come bearing receipts, demanding restitution.

We are not asking for permission to sit at your table. We are reclaiming the table itself—and every chair built on our backs. We will feast on the future we have sown with sacrifice.

The God of justice has heard our cries and the cries of our ancestors. He is not confused. He is not complicit. He is the architect of our uprising and the cornerstone of our rebuilding.

So let every city, every state, and every institution take note: We are not waiting for permission. We are rising with power. We are planting what was uprooted. We are rebuilding what was razed. And this time— we are keeping the keys.

We are not asking for favors. We are demanding a reckoning. Because the damage is not dead. It is living. It is measurable. It is systemic. And justice delayed has never been justice delivered.

We, the descendants of those who were enslaved, do not need saving. We need repair.

Let the current generation hear this clearly: We will no longer accept excuses from those who claim innocence because they were not the original perpetrators. If you are living off the fruit of stolen seed, then you are holding stolen inheritance. This nation still benefits from the foundation built by chained hands. And silence is not absolution. Silence is participation.

We will not accept pacifying policies disguised as progress. We are not infants needing comfort. We are heirs demanding our portion. We are hungry—and not for handouts, but for harvest. We are hungry for justice that nourishes a people into perpetuity. The time for appeasement is over. The time for action is now.

This is the soil of our struggle—but it is also the ground of our growth. And now, we plant something worthy of the weight we carry.

The seeds have been sown. The harvest is justice. Will you answer the call?

Because here is the truth they never teach in history books: I am a daughter of the Confederacy too. Not by allegiance, but by blood.

The same fields that fed their fortunes were watered by the sweat of my ancestors. The same land that crowned them with privilege cradled both our histories—intertwined, inseparable, and undeniable.

Their sons and daughters were born into inheritance. We were born into resistance. But the bloodline runs through us all.

We are kin—whether we confess it or not. We are stitched together by blood, by soil, by sorrow, and by survival. Bound not just by geography, but by the sacred, complicated ache of a shared past and a shared responsibility.

We cannot undo what was done. But we can decide what we build next.

It is time for a new normal—one that is not built on denial, nor on nostalgia for the days of injustice. It must be built on truth. It must be rooted in reconciliation. It must be woven with the fierce, unbreakable threads that bind us together—threads stronger than any lie, any law, or any division that ever tried to tear us apart.

We cannot afford to raise new monuments to old lies. We must become living memorials to what is possible when family refuses to keep bleeding for the past.

A new house must rise from this wounded land. A house with dignity as its foundation. A house with justice as its frame. A house with truth stretched like a roof over every name and every story.

And this time, we will build it together. The blood running through our veins demands it. The soil beneath our feet cries out for it. The future our children deserve depends on it.

We are daughters of the Confederacy. We are sons of the survivors. We are family—whether by force or by faith. And together, we will plant something worthy of the blood that has already been spilled.

The seeds have been planted. The reckoning has begun. And from these fields—justice will rise.

APPENDIX

1. The following is how I arrived at the calculation stated in the Declaration of Demand for Reparations. If the government in 1865 had given all former slaves $500 each to right the wrongs done against them, that would have been an honorable act; therefore, we will assume this amount.

2. The following reveals the method I used: I am using the time value of money to calculate what $500 issued in 1865 would be worth today—160 years later. In order to soften the blow, the final step I employ (but don't have to) is to apply core inflation against the total, which is currently at 2.8 percent. The calculation is: $FV = PV * (1 + i)^n$. PV is the initial value of what would have been given in 1865, i= the interest rate if invested in the market, and n= the number of years, which is 160. As it relates to solving what the future value of $500 is, it is applied as follows: $= \$500 * (1+.05)^{160}$. This gives us a total of $1,228,168.22. Then we multiply that amount by 2.8 percent which equals approximately $34,389. This amount is very conservative when we consider the real value of investing

in land, cotton, sugar, and tobacco over several generations, and what it would have yielded would be far greater than if it had been divided by the inflation rate.

3. In addition, historical records show that Civil War pensions for veterans and their descendants (the last of which received payouts as late as 2020) were approximately $73 per month. Over twelve months, that equals $876 per year and if you calculate that amount over 155 years of payments being paid out to descendants, we come to a total payout per person of $135,780.

4. If we combine $34,389 plus $135,780 per person, we demand payment of $170,169 per descendant of the transatlantic slave trade's enslaved persons to be set up in an established Trust that will be managed by us, for us.

5. The Commission for oversight of the Freedom Sovereign Wealth Fund (FSWF): The Commission will comprise a total of 1200 people who are chosen by our community from among us—600 qualified (vetted) financial planners who are descendants of slaves and 600 chosen as state representatives, who are also descendants of the enslaved. Each state will have 12 vetted financial planners assigned and 12 vetted representatives who will meet quarterly. The entire body of representatives will meet twice a year to set or amend policies and procedures, as well as discuss budgetary concerns. Each planner and/or representative will serve one two-year term to ensure the integrity of the fund, its distribution, and transparency to our people at large. In the last 6 months of their term, they will prepare their successor so that the new representative will understand all procedures.

6. In addition to The Commission for the FSWF, we will form a 9-member Investment Committee that will approve all investment decisions.

7. We want all allies in this movement to understand what we mean when we say "covenant." Here is our definition for it. Covenant is not transactional—it is transformational. It looks like shifting capital—not just buying once during Black History Month. It is accomplished by restructuring supply chains, choosing Black vendors, Black banks, Black developers, Black-led institutions, and hiring Black people in your organizations as key decisionmakers as part of long-term commitments. It looks like mentorship that doesn't condescend but collaborates. It looks like contracts awarded not for optics, but because repair demands redistribution. It requires partnership that transforms people, communities, organizations, businesses, and governments.

TABLE
OF FIGURES

FIGURE 1

This is the June 7, 1880 Census roll showing Hilliard and Emma living among other Black people (former slaves) in Letohatchee, AL

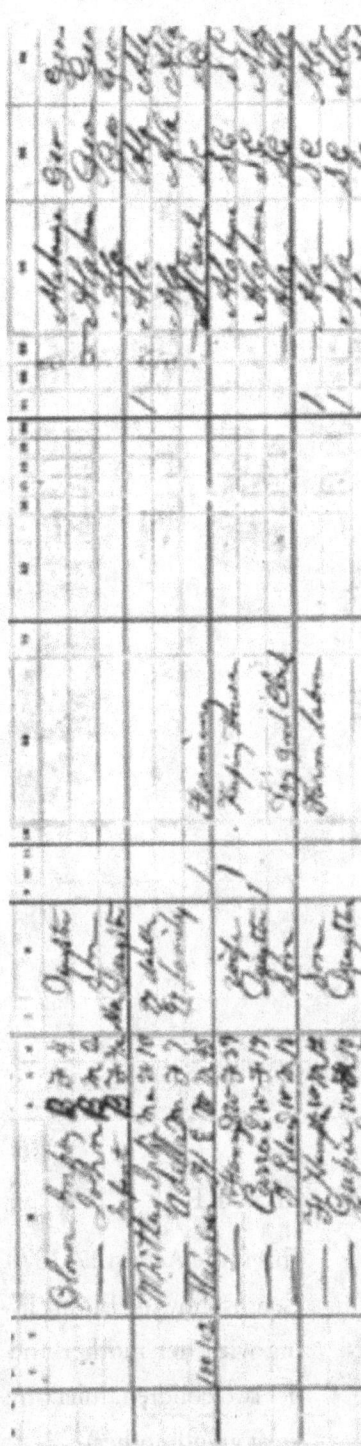

FIGURE 2

A continuation of the 1880 Census roll-my great-grandmother and her sister appear with the Glovers, just after Emma and Hilliard.

FIGURE 3

This is the August 17, 1870 Census showing Emma living with her mother and her two children, Julia (my great grandmother).

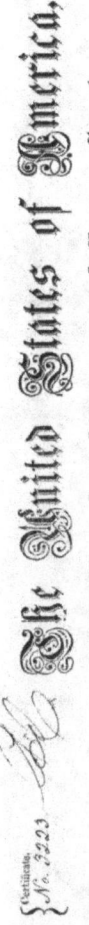

FIGURE 4

This is proof that Hilliard's father, David received farm land in Cahaba Alabama,
which is outside of Selma. It represents 79 of the 164 acres that he received in 1828.

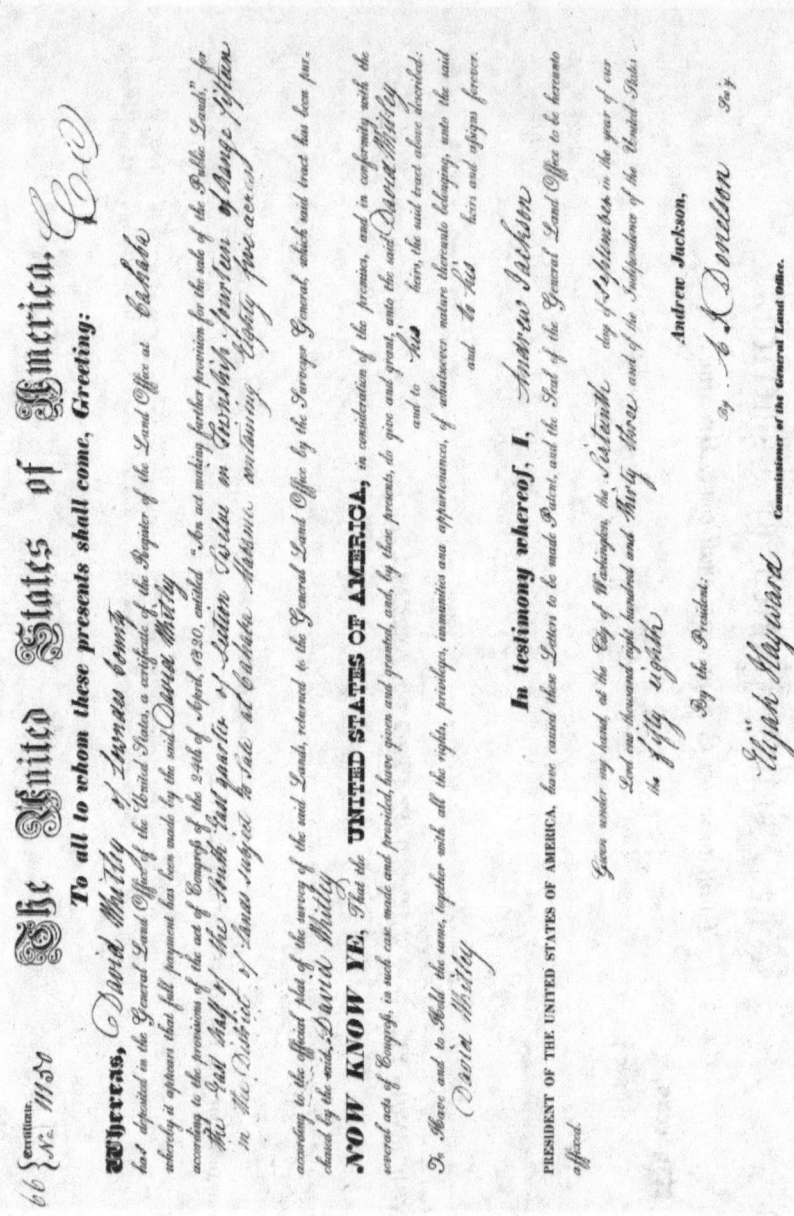

FIGURE 5

This is proof that Hilliard's father, David received farm land in Cahaba Alabama, which is outside of Selma. It includes an additional 85 acres that he received in 1833. This brought the total to 164 acres.

The State of Alabama)
Lowndes County   ¶ KNOW ALL MEN BY THESE PRESENTS:

That I, Hilliard J.Whitley of Letohatchie Alabama in the county of Lowndes and State of
Alabama, being of sound and disposing mind do hereby make and publish this my last will
and testament hereby revoking all former wills,by me at any time heretofore made.

As to my worldly estate and all the real personal or mixed property of which I shall die
seized and possessed or to which I may be entitled at the time of my decease I devise
bequeath and dispose thereof in the manner following, to-wit:

FIRST:- My will is that all my just debts and funeral expenses shall by my executor here-
inafter named be paid out of my estate as soon after my decease as convenient.

Second:- I give devise and bequeath to my sister Susan C.McDonald of Jefferson County,
Alabama, One Hundred dollars in cash.

Third:- I give devise and bequeath to Julia Carson one mule now in her possession, provided
said mule is my property at the time of my decease.

Fourth: I give devise and bequeath to my nephew D.C.Whitley one sorel horse name
"Twister" provided said horse is my property at the time of my death.

FIFTH:- I give devise and bequeath to Minnie Long Fifty dollars in cash and my large trunk.

SIXTH:- I give devise and bequeath to Lewis Jenkins(Son of A.J.Jenkins) One Hundred dollars
in cash.

SEVENTH:- All the rest of my estate real, personal or mixed of which I shall die seized and
possessed or to which I shall be entitled at my decease,I give devise and bequeath to be
equally divided between Julia Carson,and Lewis Jenkins (Son of A.J.Jenkins)

Eighth:- I do hereby nominate and appoint my friend Andrew J.Jenkins to be my executor
of this my last will and testament, and I do hereby relieve him from giving any bond,or
making accounting to the probate Court,or any other Court except to probate this my last
will and testament.

In testimony whereof, I Hilliard J.Whitley have to this my last will and testament subscribed my name and affixed my seal in the presence of the witnesses hereto,This the 23rd day
of S eptember.1907.   Hilliard J.Whitley (Seal)

Signed and published as this the last will and testament of the said Hilliard J.Whitley
in our presence and in the presence of each other at his request and we each hereunto
subscribe our names as witnesses on the day and date of said will.
                                        S.D.Suggs.
                                        N.M.Bayner.

The State of Alabama)
Lowndes County   )Probate Court.

In the matter of the probate and record of the last will and testament of H.J.Whitley,
deceased. Before me J.C.Wood, Judge of probate Court in and for the county and State aforesaid,personally appeared in open Court N.M.Bayner who having been by me first duly sworn
and examined, did and does depose and say that S.D.Suggs and himself are subscribing witnesses to the foregoing instrument of writing, now shown to the said affiant, and which
purports to be the last will and testament of H.J.Whitley deceased, late an inhabitant of
this county, that the said H.J.Whitley since deceased, signed and executed said instrument
on the day the same bears date, and declared the same to be his last will and testament, and
that affiant set his signature thereto, on the day the same bears date,as subscribing
witness to the same, in the presence of the testator and at his request, and in the presence of each other, and that said testator was of sound mind and disposing memory and understanding, and in the opinion of affiant fully capable of making his said last will and
at the time the same was so made, as aforesaid, And deponent further states that said testator was, on the day of the date of said will, of the full age of twenty one years and
upward, and a resident of this county.   N.M.Bayner.
Subscribed and sworn to before me this 11th day of May A.D.1908.
                        J.C.Wood Judge of probate Court Lowndes County.

The State of Alabama)
Lowndes County   ) I, J.C.Wood Judge of the probate Court in and for the county and
State aforesaid do hereby certify that the within instrument of writing has this day in said
Court, and before me as the Judge thereof, been duly proven by the testimony of N.M.Bayner
subscribing witness, to be the genuine last will and testament of Hilliard J.Whitley,deceas-
ed, and that said will together with the proof thereof has been recorded in my office in
Book Number D of wills at page 67.In witness whereof, I have hereunto set my hand and af-
fixed the seal of the said probate Court on this the 11th day of May A.D. One Thousand
Nine Hundred and eight.
            J.C.Wood Judge of the Probate Court Lowndes County. Alabama.

FIGURE 6

This is Hilliard's Last Will (September 1907) where he included my great grandmother, Julia Carson, in it. He had no land or other real assets.

ACKNOWLEDGMENTS

If you've made it to this page, thank you. Not just for reading—but for *witnessing*.

What you held in your hands was more than fiction. It was a composite of truth, memory, prayer, prophecy and protest. It was the weaving of what was, what is, and what could still be—if we are courageous enough to confront it.

The story of Hilliard and Emma was never just theirs. It is emblematic of what so many have lived and lost, buried and borne. It is the tension between who America says it is, and who it has been to those of us whose stories were carved into the margins. In telling their story, I also told part of mine. And perhaps part of yours, too.

I did not write this book to entertain. I wrote it to unearth what has been buried beneath silence and shame. I put pen to paper to disturb those who have grown too comfortable in systems of injustice. I wrote it to comfort those who carry wounds the world refuses to see. I wrote it to hold sacred space for truth, for reckoning, and for healing.

So, if you felt something shift while reading—an ache, a revelation, a question you can't unask—lean in. That's the Holy Spirit stirring the soil of your heart.

I pray this book has given voice to what was once silent. I pray it makes room for lament, but also for hope. And I pray it gives you the language—and the boldness—to speak your own truth in the face of history's denials.

We are the descendants of both greatness and grief. We are the children of both promise and pain. But above all, we are *not forgotten*.

The God of justice sees. The God of mercy restores. And the work of repair is holy work.

Let the work continue.

With much appreciation, peace, and love,
—*Lauraine White*

ABOUT THE AUTHOR

Lauraine White is a prophetic storyteller, author, speaker, and truth-teller whose words echo with both anointing and ancestral memory. With a voice rooted in faith and sharpened by lived experience, Lauraine writes at the intersection of history, identity, and redemption—calling forth a generation to remember, reckon, and rise.

Born in the South and shaped by both the wounds and wonders of her heritage, Lauraine is no stranger to struggle. She is the author of *Chosen*, a deeply personal memoir chronicling her spiritual awakening and the hard-won lessons of obedience. Her follow-up works, *The Way Out* and *Bulletproof*, further established her as a bold voice in Christian literature—equipping believers with spiritual insight, warfare strategies, and the courage to confront both internal and external strongholds.

Lauraine holds a master's degree from Georgetown University, is a licensed real estate broker in the state of Georgia and has served as Vice President in the banking industry. A lifelong entrepreneur and real estate investor, she has also founded her own publishing company and produced transformational masterclasses, including *The Way Out Master Class* and *Bulletproof Master Class*.

But her deepest work is in truth-telling—unearthing the silenced stories of Black America and confronting the whitewashed myths that still dominate our national conscience. *A Daughter of the Confederacy* is her most courageous offering to date: a historical work, a prophetic lament, a love story, and a national reckoning all woven into one. With lyrical depth and prophetic urgency, Lauraine brings voice to the unheard and visibility to the unseen.

She lives by the belief that writing is not just expression—it is intercession. Her pen is prayer, prophecy, protest, and purpose.

Lauraine White is a mother, a mentor, a messenger—and a daughter of both the dream and the dirt. Through every page, she invites readers to confront the past, embrace healing, and co-labor with God in the sacred work of restoration.

You can learn more about her books, teachings, and ministry at

MIRACLE-MOVEMENT.COM

www.ingramcontent.com/pod-product-compliance
Lightning Source LLC
Chambersburg PA
CBHW011221120626
46545CB00010B/3097